Coping With Conflict

A Resource Book for the Middle School Years

Frances Mary Nicholas

Learning Development Aids

Coping with Conflict
LD 794
ISBN 0 905 114 264
© Text Francis Mary Nicholas
© Cartoons by John Woodgates
Designed, illustrated and produced by E.A.R.O.

First published 1987
Reprinted 1991

LDA, Duke Street, Wisbech, Cambs. PE13 2AE, England

CONTENTS

APPENDICES

LIST OF INFORMATION AND ACTIVITY SHEETS

Acknowledgements

Thanks are due to the following for permission to reproduce copyright material:

Leonard Bird and the Northern Friends Peace Board, for quotations from *Costa Rica – A Country without an Army*;

Philadelphia Yearly Meeting of the Religious Society of Friends, for activities from *For the Fun of it*, reproduced by Pax Christi in *Winners All*;

Priscilla Prutzman *et al* and Avery, New Jersey, for activities from *The Friendly Classroom for a Small Planet*;

Quaker Peace and Service for the *Donkeys* poster.

INTRODUCTION

This is a practical book for everyone who is involved in the education of groups of 9–13 year-olds. It is designed to be flexible, so that it can be used both by class teachers employing an integrated approach and by subject teachers working to a timetable. It spans many of the traditional subjects such as English, Drama, Geography, Religious Education, Maths and Art and hence provides an excellent basis for project or topic work in a junior or middle school. It is also well suited to the teaching of Humanities, Social Studies, Personal and Social Education, World Studies and Religious Education in a middle or secondary school. Much of the material could, with little modification, be used in situations outside school, such as youth and church groups.

The book deals with issues of conflict and co-operation, violence and peace. It also looks at opportunities for choice and change and at our hopes and fears for the future.

Why study such issues with children? Conflict is an important element in children's lives. They experience it in arguments at home, in quarrels or fights at school and in violence portrayed in the media. They also meet it in history, social studies and many other parts of the school curriculum. If they are to cope well with life they need to understand and deal successfully with a range of conflicts. The book encourages children to look at conflicts both within their own experience and in the wider world and to explore different ways of resolving them. It helps them understand the consequences of violence and the real possibilities of non-violent approaches. Making choices and bringing about change also involve us in conflicts. The book helps children to consider how the future is shaped by the choices we make, and gives them the opportunity to discuss their hopes and fears for the future.

The activities are designed to stimulate children to ask questions and solve problems for themselves. The book tries to involve them in the processes of thinking and feeling which can lead them to understand conflict and change in the world around them. It is hoped that children will both discover new facts about their world and develop new attitudes and skills which may help them to live in harmony with their neighbours.

The material is divided into four main parts:

PART A: SMALL WORLD starts with the children's immediate experience. Through drama, games and role play it explores co-operation and conflict at first hand.

PART B: WIDER WORLD looks at conflict and violence which children experience at second hand, through the media.

PART C: OTHERS' WORLDS moves further afield to other cultures. It looks first at our prejudices towards foreigners and then at three societies with attitudes to aggression and war very different from our own.

PART D: OUR WORLD considers change and our power to influence it, and illustrates the possibility of achieving change through non-violent action. It also looks at different possible scenarios for the future.

Each of these parts has two sections. Within each section there are pages addressed to the teacher and others, marked 'Information Sheet' or 'Activity Sheet', addressed to the children. Those for the teacher provide background information and describe activities which the children can undertake. Those for the children give information, pose questions for discussion and suggest activities such as writing, drama and artwork. These pages may be photocopied for distribution. A few of them are addressed primarily to the older or more able children in the 9–13 age range, but these can be adapted for younger or less able children.

How the book came to be written

Coping with Conflict is based on a teaching pack entitled *Conflict, Change and our Future* which was produced by a group of teachers and others meeting at the Norwich Teachers' Centre. The group was part of the Council for Educational Technology's "County Links" project. The teaching pack was based on the practical experience of the group members and developed from accounts of successful sessions that they had undertaken with children. The pack was accompanied by a collection of picture postcards with questions for discussion* and a set of four co-operative board games designed by Peter Brimblecombe. This book retains the basic approach and much of the subject matter of the original teaching pack, but it has been completely rewritten and new material has been added.

Thanks are due firstly to Quaker Peace and Service which gave a great deal of financial and practical support to the present author while she was working on the original teaching pack. The Norwich Teachers' Centre also played a key part in making the production of this book possible by enabling the working group to make use of its facilities. Thanks go particularly to its co-ordinator, John Jennings, for his encouragement, enthusiasm and practical help. The book is the result of the efforts of a large number of people, too numerous for them all to be mentioned by name. The original authors are listed below, as are the people who kindly read through drafts of various sections and made invaluable suggestions. Special thanks are due also to Peter Brimblecombe, to Jim Embling and the Council for Educational Technology, to Norwich Quaker Meeting and to Mike Marriage and other staff at the Norwich City College Computer Centre.

Authors who have contributed to the book:
Peter Brimblecombe
Sister Doreen SND
Anne Filgate
Michael Filgate
Elizabeth Hoffbauer
Elizabeth Masterton
Lorraine Mullings
Grace Ogilvie
Jon Oram
Alan Reed
Frances Warns
Brian Watson
Tony Williams
David Wright
Dene Zarins
Angela Zelter

Readers who have commented on various drafts:
Ian Breckenridge
Peter Brimblecombe
David Chapman
Ruth Garwood
Derick Last
Barry Nicholas
Hildegart Nicholas
Roger Whittaker
Maxine Wood

* This picture set *Peace, Conflict and Violence* is available from EARO, The Resource Centre, Back Hill, Ely, Cambs CB7 4DA.

PART A   SMALL WORLD

This part of the book focuses on the small world of the children's immediate experience. It aims to help children deal with the kinds of conflicts they experience every day. Before any of us can learn to resolve such conflicts creatively, we need to have had experience of co-operating with one another. The first section suggests various activities which can help to develop co-operation skills and thus lay foundations for tackling conflict resolution. The second section looks at the kinds of conflicts children commonly experience and encourages them to explore a variety of methods of resolving such conflicts.

SECTION 1 LEARNING TO CO-OPERATE

If people are to co-operate, they need to respect and trust one another. It is difficult to co-operate with others if one is feeling angry, fearful or rejected. So the first step in developing co-operation skills is to encourage children to feel positive towards themselves and others, and to appreciate the good qualities in themselves and in other people. They also need the ability to communicate. This of course involves listening to others and understanding them as well as being able to convey one's own thoughts and feelings accurately. Self-esteem and communication skills provide the basis for co-operation, and learning to co-operate is an important step in learning to deal with conflict.

Obviously there are many different ways of developing confidence, communication and co-operation. Any activity in which children have some measure of responsibility and work together towards a common goal will tend to do so. Preparing a meal together or running a school garden would be examples of projects which might develop these attitudes and skills, but this unit concentrates on activities which can be completed in short periods of time. It provides ideas for simple games and activities which develop the attitudes and skills necessary for creative conflict resolution.

A large variety of ideas has been included so that you can choose those most suitable for your class. If you are working with older children you may feel that some of the games are too childish for them. Obviously no-one would want to play all the games described here one after another, but those not used the first time round can be returned to later on. Many of the activities would be best carried out in a drama lesson or on some other occasion when a fairly large space is available. However, those marked with an asterisk can also be played in the classroom, and those marked with two asterisks are specifically intended for the classroom.

For many of the ideas in this section the author is indebted to the New York 'Children's Creative Response to Conflict Program' and the Philadelphia 'Non-violence and Children Program'. Further activities and also background information and philosophy are to be found in the books by Judson and Prutzman listed under 'Further Resources'.

Lesson ideas for the teacher	Activity sheets for the children
1.1 Warm-ups	
1.2 Confidence-building activities	
1.3 Communication games	Pictures for the drawing game
1.4 Co-operation games	Co-operation pictures
1.5 Trust games	

Further Resources for the Teacher

Andrew Fluegelman (ed), *The New Games Book*, Sidgwick and Jackson, 1978.

*Stephanie Judson (ed), *A Manual on Non-violence and Children*, Non-violence and Children Program, Philadelphia Friends Peace Committee, 1977.

* Available from Housmans Bookshop

3

Mildred Masheder, *Let's Co-operate: Activities and Ideas for Parents and Teachers of Young Children*, Peace Education Project, 1986.

Terry Orlick, *The Co-operative Sports and Games Book*, Writers and Readers Publishing Co-operative, 1979.

Pax Christi, *Winners All*, Pax Christi, 1980.

*Priscilla Prutzman *et al*, *The Friendly Classroom for a Small Planet*, Avery, 1978.

Anna Scher and Charles Verrall, *100+ Ideas for Drama*, Heinemann Educational Books, 1975.

Jim Wingate, *How to be a peace-full teacher*, Friendly Press, 1985.

* Available from Housmans Bookshop

1.1 WARM-UPS

These games are useful for helping children to feel at ease and to become involved in a group at the beginning of a session.

Loosening-up game

This is a simple theatre warm-up exercise. It helps create a high energy level and prepares children for sketches and role playing. Stand in front of a group and ask the children to imitate the sounds and motions that you make. The sillier you look, the more you help produce an atmosphere that is comfortable and low-risk for everyone else. Once everyone understands how the exercise works, ask others to lead with sounds and motions.

Name game 1

This may be useful at the beginning of the year to help children learn each other's names. Ask everyone to stand in a circle. Take something soft (eg a small cushion or a scarf/jumper tied up into a ball) and throw it to someone while calling your name. This person then throws it to someone else while calling their own name, and so the game continues. Once everyone has had time to become familiar with a reasonable number of names, the game changes so that instead of saying your own name as you throw, you call the name of the person to whom you are throwing. Names can be asked if people forget them, as this is not meant to be a memory test, but simply an enjoyable way of learning names.

Name game 2

This is a good co-operative game at any time, though it may be particularly useful at the beginning of the year. It begins in the same way as Name game 1, except that from the start you call the name of the person to whom you are throwing. Each person is to receive the ball once only, and people are asked to remember from whom they received it and to whom they threw it. (Names can be asked.) Towards the end you will probably have to ask who has not yet had the ball. The last person throws it back to you. The throwing is then repeated quickly in the same order, with names being called out as before.

Next, four more 'balls' are introduced and thrown in succession to follow the first one, always proceeding from person to person in the original order. After this, two of the balls (which must be easily distinguishable from the others) are thrown round in the opposite direction, while the remaining balls are thrown in the original direction. Names should always accompany throws.

With younger children you may want to limit the number of balls to three and simply to reverse the direction of the throwing rather than throwing in two directions at once.

*Name game 3

This name game has the advantage that it can be played anywhere. It is best if everyone can sit in a circle, but this is not essential. The first person introduces herself by saying her name preceeded by an adjective which starts with the same letter and which says something positive about her, eg 'I am joyful Jenny'. The next person says eg 'This is joyful Jenny and I am gentle George'. The third person introduces the first two and then himself in the same way. If the group is small, each person can repeat all the names, but if it is large it may be better for each person simply to introduce the two people before him and himself. Tell the group that if they forget names they can simply ask.

Variation   If you want to get people laughing, encourage them to choose ridiculous adjectives to introduce themselves eg 'Juicy Julian'.

Herman Henrietta

Herman Henrietta is an imaginary blob of clay that can be shaped into anything. With the children in a circle, begin miming by pulling the imaginary blob from your pocket and set the tone of the game by seriously beginning to create something. To start with it is a good idea to create something very simple that the children can identify easily. It is fun to guess the object, but not necessary, as the aim of the game is quiet concentration on what another person is doing. After you have finished, press the magical lump down to its original size and pass it reverently to the next person. The game continues around the circle.

Farmyard

This is a noisy game which can help shy children to drop some of their inhibitions and join in the group. Cut a slip of paper for each child and write on each slip the name of an animal. It is best to have about four of each animal eg four slips of paper will say 'cat'. However, if the group is smaller than sixteen you will need about three of each animal, and if it is larger than twenty-eight, about five of each animal. Hand out the slips of paper. The children must then close their eyes and walk slowly around the room, constantly calling out in the call of their own kind (*Baa Baa, Meow Meow etc*). When two animals of one kind come across each other they should hold hands and find others of their kind until the group is complete. The object of the game is not to finish first, but merely to find others of your own kind.

* For hall or classroom

1.2 CONFIDENCE-BUILDING ACTIVITIES

If we acknowledge and appreciate each other's qualities and abilities this helps to build up self-confidence. Having a sense of self-esteem helps us to feel less threatened in conflict situations and enables us to see the good in others, including those with whom we are in conflict. The activities suggested here encourage children to build up their own and each other's self-confidence.

*Opening circle

Activities in which people are together in a circle tend to encourage an atmosphere of openness and trust, especially if people can be sufficiently unselfconscious to hold hands. 'Opening Circle' is particularly suitable for younger children. Everyone is given the opportunity to tell the others something new and good that has happened to them since the group last met, something that they are pleased about. It can be something very small eg 'I saw a woodpecker on the way to school', or something bigger eg 'I got a new bicycle for my birthday'. Although everyone should be encouraged to say something, no-one should be forced to do so.

**Poster Choice

This helps children to feel confident in expressing their opinions. It requires a display of some kind, for instance a selection of posters or cartoons. Ask each child to select three items from the display according to some criterion which you suggest. For instance, you might ask them to choose the three which they would like best on their bedroom wall, or which they find funniest or most interesting. It is important that this choice should be a personal one, arrived at without discussion. Next, each child finds a partner and the two explain their choices to each other. They then, as a pair, repeat the exercise so that they agree on three items between them. Each pair then meets up with another pair and the whole process is repeated once more. The final stage is to try and identify which three or so items in the display have received the most 'votes' from the class as a whole.

Mime one thing you like to do

This game encourages confidence in the individual and helps to build up a group feeling. Form a large circle and ask children in turn to mime one thing they like to do. Be sure to let people finish their mimes before others start to guess what they are doing. Everyone who wants to do a mime should have a chance.

** For classroom

**Personal notebooks

This encourages individuals to feel positive about themselves and their lives. Each child is to create a little book about him/herself, preferably stressing the positive aspects of his/her life. You can suggest things to write about or draw pictures of eg 'Things I like to do', 'A description of myself as I would like to be in ten years' time'. The children can also use the book as a kind of diary in which they record good things that happen to them, and they can design their own notebook covers. It is important not to insist that you see everything in the notebooks, otherwise the children may not feel able to write or draw freely.

* For hall or classroom

1.3 COMMUNICATION GAMES

People cannot co-operate and resolve conflicts unless they can understand what the other person or group is saying. This means that both sides need to be able to express themselves clearly and accurately and to listen carefully and openly to each other. The ability to take in information with one's eyes as well as one's ears and to express oneself non-verbally also improves understanding and communication. The following activities are designed to help children develop the range of skills they need in order to communicate effectively.

**Rumour

This game encourages skills of observation and expression. Ask a volunteer to leave the room, and then show a fairly complicated picture to those remaining. Ask them to look at it carefully so that they can describe it later. Then put the picture away and ask the person outside to return. The rest of the class describes to this person what they saw in the picture.

Usually there are several different versions of what the picture contained and this can lead to a discussion of how and why our observations vary. If this game is played several times, observation skills should improve.

A more complicated way of playing the game is to have two people go out of the room. Bring the first one back as before and have the group describe the picture. Then bring the second person back and ask the first person to describe to the second what s/he heard. This can lead to a useful discussion of how rumours get started.

*Listening

Get everyone to sit (or lie) quietly and comfortably. First ask them to listen to all the sounds they can hear coming from outside the building. After a minute or two, ask them to bring their attention to sounds emanating from inside the building, and after this to sounds from inside the room, and finally to those within themselves. Afterwards the children can talk about what they have heard. This can lead to a discussion of how one can choose what to hear, and how much we miss in the usual bustle. Do we all have the same choice about what we hear? (What about people with hearing aids?) When do the children usually experience silence? When and where do they like or dislike it?

**Instructions game

This can be a lot of fun and can help children learn to give accurate instructions. Ask the class to give you detailed instructions to perform a simple task, like watering the classroom plants, as if you had no idea how to do it. Obey all instructions as literally and stupidly as possible. For instance, if asked to get some water, get it in your hand; if asked to take a jug, hold it by the spout. Once your task is completed, children can take it in turns to be the one to obey instructions.

** For classroom

9

**Drawing game

This game encourages accurate listening to and giving of instructions. It can be adapted to suit different levels of ability, but some understanding of mathematical language is required.

One person gives step-by-step drawing instructions to others without telling them what is being drawn. If the instructions are good and if those who are drawing carry them out accurately they should all end up with recognisable pictures.

Two sample sets of instructions are given here. The first uses simple language, though if the children have compasses or protractors the instructions could be rewritten more economically. The second is quite complex and suitable only for children with a good grasp of the mathematical concepts and language involved.

Instructions for a simple drawing (the teepee):

1 Draw a straight line across the bottom of your page, about 14 cm long.
2 With a soft pencil, lightly mark the following points on the line, writing the letters below the line:
   Point A – 2 cm from the end of the line
   Point B – 5 cm from the end of the line
   Point C – 7 cm from the end of the line
   Point D – 9 cm from the end of the line
   Point E – 12 cm from the end of the line
3 Lay your ruler at right angles to the line and passing through point C. Mark a point F 3 cm above the line and a point G 10 cm above it.
4 Join point A to point G
   Join point E to point G
   Join point B to point F
   Join point D to point F
5 Extend the line AG another 2 cm beyond G.
   Extend the line EG another 2 cm beyond G
6 Rub out the letters.

The drawing should look like this:

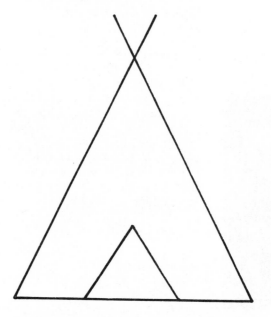

* For hall or classroom

Instructions for a complex drawing (the cat):

1 Draw a circle at least 5 cm in diameter.
2 From the centre of the circle draw downwards within it, a large letter J.
3 Draw a mirror image of the letter J starting from the same point and drawing downwards.
4 Draw a horizontal diameter across the circle and extend it a little beyond the circumference at both ends.
5 Draw another diameter about 20 degrees to the horizontal and again extend it just beyond the circumference at both ends.
6 Draw a third diameter about 20 degrees from the horizontal in the opposite direction and extend the ends as before.
7 Above these diameters on the left and still inside the circle, draw an upside-down capital U.
8 Draw another U in a similar position on the right.
9 Underneath each U put a dot.
10 Outside the circle, resting on its circumference, draw upside down capital V's above the U's.

The result should look like the drawing on the left, though many probably will not!

The children can now try to devise their own sets of instructions. Let the class divide into small groups and give each child a simple picture. You could use the pictures on p. 13. Ask the children to write instructions for drawing the picture you have given them. When they have done so they should take turns to give their instructions to the others in their group. It is of course very important that the children cannot see each other's pictures.

If the children are keen to try drawing their own pictures, you could let them do so, but you will need to emphasize the importance of drawing simple geometrical shapes which can easily be explained.

**Drawing with a computer

The drawing game can be played by giving instructions to a computer rather than to other people. This definitely requires the child to give full and accurate instructions, since the computer will not fill in any gaps in the instructions as a person might. Examples are given here of how one might draw a teepee using various computer languages, though obviously the children should try to write their own instructions. The cricket bat would be another fairly simple picture for which they could write instructions.

Instructions for drawing a teepee:

On a computer like AMSTRAD PCW 8265 the proceedural language DR. LOGO can be used. This is an excellent language for children because the resulting movement of the 'turtle' can immediately be seen on the screen. The instructions might look like this:

```
setpos [-200 0]
setpos [200 0]
setpos [70 0]
setpos [-10 210]
pu
setpos [10 210]
pd
setpos [-70 0]
setpos [-20 0]
setpos [0 60]
setpos [20 0]
```

Programming in BASIC for the BBC Computer might look something like this:

```
10 CLS
20 MOVE 100,100
30 DRAW 600,100
40 MOVE 370,625
50 DRAW 200,100
60 MOVE 330,625
70 DRAW 500,100
80 MOVE 400,100
90 DRAW 350,300
100 DRAW 300,100
```

In a programming language such as MSX-BASIC or GW-BASIC a program to draw a teepee might look like this:

```
5 CLS
15 LINE (50,100)–(250,100)
25 LINE (200,100)–(145,25)
35 LINE (155,25)–(100,100)
45 LINE (140,100)–(150,75)
55 LINE (160,100)–(150,75)
```

*Back-writing

This introduces an unusual form of communication. The children work in pairs and take turns to communicate a word or a short sentence to their partners by using their fingers to write it on their partners' backs. This can develop into a conversation.

Gibberish talking

This develops skills of non-linguistic communication. Divide the children into pairs or small groups and give them a situation on which to improvise. They must do their improvisation using sounds rather than recognisable words. You could suggest that they should imagine they are talking a foreign language. Or you could introduce the idea of gibberish language beforehand by reading and discussing Lewis Carroll's poem *Jabberwocky* (from the first chapter of *Through the Looking Glass*).

Mime conversations

These develop skills of silent communication. The children work in pairs and hold conversations without sound. Words can be mimed, gestured or even mouthed (though too much mouthing should be discouraged). You can either let the children make up their own conversations, or you can write sentences on slips of paper and hand them out. It sometimes helps to set a time limit.

*For hall or classroom

PICTURES FOR THE DRAWING GAME

1.4 CO-OPERATION GAMES

These activities encourage co-operation by creating situations in which people have to work together. Most of the situations are relatively free of conflict, but in the last two games the participants have to use co-operative strategies to overcome apparent conflicts of interest.

Machine building

This game encourages co-operation which involves physical contact. Working in groups of about five, the children try to represent a machine with each child miming a part (preferably a moving part). Ask one child in each group to start by miming some repetitive movement and let the others join in one by one. This could be done to music which has a regular rhythm. When they have grasped the idea of creating a machine in this spontaneous way, they could try discussing what kind of machine they want to make before they start miming. The machine could be imaginary, allowing scope for creativity in the where's and how's of the moving parts. Or it could be a real machine, in which case the fun lies in trying to work out how to use people to represent the parts.

Note: Physically handicapped children may be able to join in this game, as a crutch or a wheelchair can be very useful and form an important part of a machine.

Limb sculptures

The children make self-supporting sculptures out of people. Different size groups can be used, and various limitations set (eg groups of six, but only five limbs touching the floor).

Passing

This is a very simple co-operative exercise, suitable especially for younger children. Ask everyone to stand in a circle, holding hands. Start the game by gently squeezing the hand of the child on your right. When s/he feels the squeeze, s/he passes it on by squeezing with his/her right hand. In this way a hand-squeeze is passed round the circle. Excessive pressure should not be used, as this destroys concentration. The game can be speeded up by sending another squeeze (perhaps in the opposite direction) while the first is on its way. Or it can be done with hand-claps (with eyes open or closed).

** For classroom

**One word at a time

This requires the children to listen to each other and create something together. The whole class, or groups or pairs, tell a story with each person contributing one word eg 'One – day – there – was – a – small – elephant . . . . . .'

Mirrors

This activity encourages sensitive co-operation. The children work in pairs facing each other. Ask them to decide who in each pair is A and who is B. Then ask A to begin slow movements while B copies as if there is an imaginary mirror between them and he is the mirror image. Thus if A raises her right hand and touches her left ear, B will raise his left hand and touch his right ear. After a few minutes ask the children to reverse roles. It is helpful for partners to have eye contact and use smooth, flowing motions. Realistic movements such as shaving or combing hair can be included. Eventually the pairs should be working so closely together that neither child is leading: both are contributing to the motion. It is a good idea to end by asking the children how they felt about the exercise.

Variations

1 Two pairs work together and use real situations (eg the barber's, the dentist's).
2 Extend the mirror activity by using sounds as well as movements. The sounds could include words, but they would need to be said in a slow and drawn-out way.
3 Introduce an exchange element in which A copies B's movements while B copies A's sounds or words.
4 Puppets: A stands on a chair behind B, who is the puppet. B leads the action, while A holds the strings and tries to look as if s/he is leading. After a while it should be difficult to see who is leading.
5 Copy Cats: The children all stand in a circle and copy one person's movements.
6 Who leads?: One person leaves the room. A leader is then selected and the group plays 'Copy Cats'. The person outside returns and has to try and identify the leader.

Pru-ee

This is a delightful activity for groups of fifteen or more. Ask everyone to close their eyes. Then whisper in someone's ear 'You're the Pru-ee.' Now everyone, including the Pru-ee, begins to mingle with eyes shut. Each person is to find another's hand and ask 'Pru-ee?' If the other person also asks 'Pru-ee?' they both drop hands and go on to someone else. Everyone goes round asking 'Pru-ee?' except the Pru-ee who remains silent the whole time. When you get no response to the question 'Pru-ee?' you know that you have found the Pru-ee and hang on to that hand. You thus becomes part of the Pru-ee and also remain silent. Anyone else shaking hands with the Pru-ee (now two people) becomes part of it, and thus it becomes larger and larger. If you find only clasped hands and silence, you can join the line at that point. Soon the cries of 'Pru-ee?' will dwindle and the Pru-ee will increase until everyone in the room is holding hands. At this point everyone is asked to open their eyes. There are usually gasps of surprise and laughter.

Note: 'Pru-ee?' sounds like a high-pitched little bird call.

Group knot

Ask the whole class to form a circle and hold hands. Break the circle at one point, thus creating two ends. Ask the end people to lead the others over and under the arches made by people's arms until the whole class is knotted together. It is essential that no-one lets go of hands, and that all movements are slow so that no-one gets hurt. When the children are thoroughly knotted together, tell them they must now untie themselves without breaking hands. Persistence may be needed!

Note: It may be unwise for children with physical injury or weakness to take part in the group knot. In that case, play the variation below and let them stay outside the circle.

Variation: Ask one or two children to stand outside the circle and close their eyes (or leave the room) while the knot is being formed. Then invite them to come and unravel the knot by instructing the others where to move.

Rainstorm

This is a good co-operative activity with which to end a session. Ask the children to stand in a circle, placing yourself in the centre. You are going to be the 'conductor' of the rainstorm. As with an orchestra, the conductor brings each person in. Stand in front of the first child and start rubbing your hands together, letting him/her follow you. Then turn slowly round on the spot rubbing your hands in front of each child in turn until they are all performing this action,

** For classroom

which should sound like gentle, and increasingly heavy, rainfall.
When you get back to the first child, change the action to snapping
fingers. As you turn round again each child changes his/her action
to copy yours, so that the storm gradually grows louder. Repeat the
whole process with a third action: slapping thighs, and then with a
fourth: stamping feet. No sooner has the rainstorm reached its peak
than it begins to die down again. Once everyone is stamping their
feet, change your actions back to slapping thighs, and gradually
decrease the volume by going through all the steps in reverse until
the last child is silent.

**Co-operation pictures

The following two games place children in a conflict situation which
cannot end until they co-operate. 'Co-operation Pictures' is a simple
version of 'Co-operation Squares', though without its subtlety and
challenge. The 'picture' version should be used with younger
children or as an introduction to the 'squares' version, though the
latter is suitable only for older or brighter children.

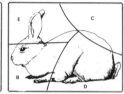

On pp. 20–24 is a set of five pictures which need to be cut into
pieces along the lines indicated. Each group of five children will
need one set of pictures, so if the whole class is to play the game at
once, further sets will have to be photocopied. For each set, mark
five envelopes A to E and put the appropriate pieces in each
envelope. Seat each group of five children at a table. Spare children
can be observers.

Give each group one set of pictures, one envelope to each child. Say
that the envelopes are not to be opened until a signal is given. Give
the following instructions:

1 Each of you has an envelope containing jigsaw pieces of pictures
  of a rabbit, but the pieces in your envelope do not fit together to
  make a complete rabbit. The task of the group is to form five
  identical rabbit pictures. In other words, you will all be trying to
  complete the five rabbits. The task is not finished until you each
  have a whole picture before you.
2 You are only allowed to give pieces to other people – and each
  piece must be given to a specific person. You are not allowed to
  take a jigsaw piece from anyone else.
3 During the game no-one may speak. You are not allowed to
  communicate in any way – by smiles, hand signals, longing
  glances etc.

When everyone has understood the instructions, give the signal to
open the envelopes.

When all groups have finished, the class should discuss their
feelings and reactions.

1 *Did they feel frustrated with the others?*
2 *Did they feel frustrated with themselves?*
3 *Were they afraid of looking foolish?*
4 *Did they find it hard not to talk?*
5 *Did they cheat?*

If there were observers they can be invited to join in the discussion by commenting on how their group functioned.

**Co-operation squares

This is a more advanced version of 'Co-operation Pictures'. Prepare sets of squares so that you have enough for one set between five. A set consists of five 30cm squares of stiff paper or card, cut up as shown below.

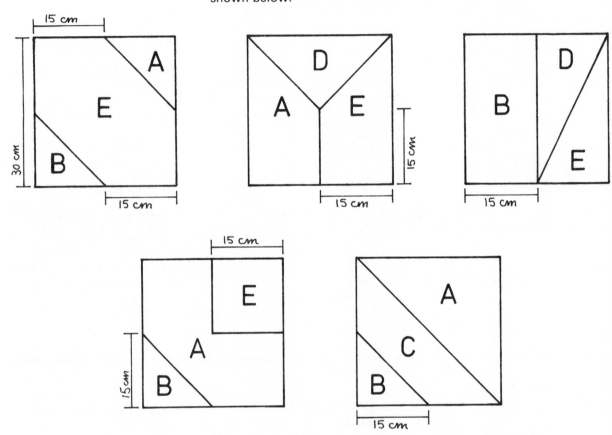

Mark five envelopes A to E, letter the pieces as shown, and put the appropriate pieces in each envelope. Divide the class into groups of five and seat each group of five children at a table. Spare children can be observers.

Give each group one set of pictures, one envelope to each child. Say that the envelopes are not to be opened until a signal is given. Give the following instructions:

1 Each of you has an envelope containing jigsaw pieces cut from large squares, but the pieces in your envelope do not fit together to make a complete square. The task of the group is to form five identical squares. In other words, you will all be trying to complete the five squares, and they are all the same size. The task is not finished until you each have a whole square before you.

2 You are only allowed to give pieces to other people – and each piece must be given to a specific person. You are not allowed to take a jigsaw piece from anyone else.

3 During the game no-one may speak. You are not allowed to communicate in any way – by smiles, hand signals, longing glances etc.

When everyone has understood the instructions, give the signal to open the envelopes.

The following questions might be helpful in provoking discussion afterwards.

1 *How did you feel?*
2 *How did the holder of envelope C feel?*
3 *Did anyone else notice that C had only one piece?*
4 *How did you feel when someone held a piece and did not see that someone else needed it?*
5 *Were you afraid you would look foolish because you couldn't see what to do?*
6 *What was your reaction when someone finished a square and then sat back without seeing if that solution prevented others from completing their squares?*
7 *Did you finish your square and then realise that you would have to break it up and give away a piece? How did you feel about that?*
8 *Did you follow the instructions? If not, how do you feel? Satisfied? Angry?*
9 *Did you see anyone else not following the instructions? What was your reaction?*
10 *How did you feel about a person who was slow at seeing the solution or who misunderstood the instructions?*
11 *What processes enabled some groups to finish quickly?*

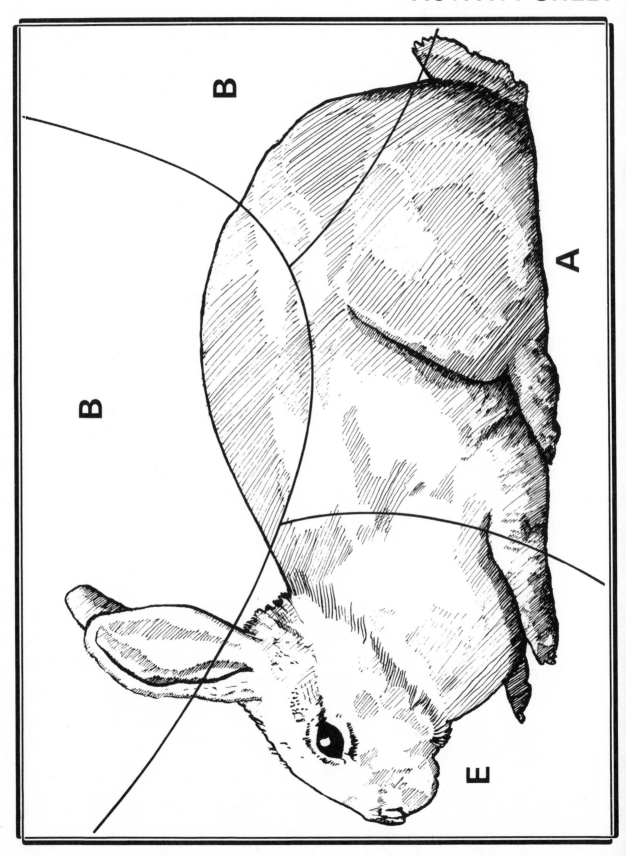

B

B

A

E

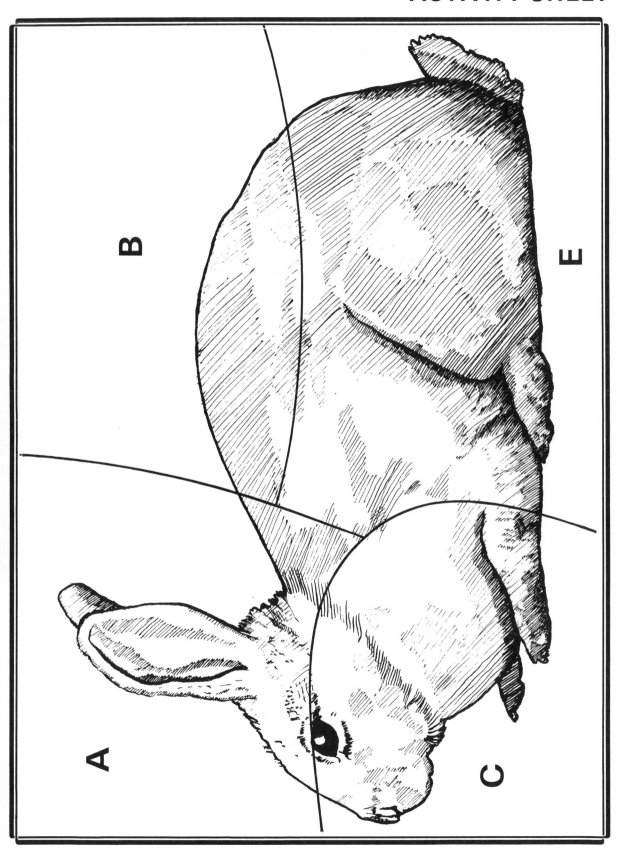

A

B

C

E

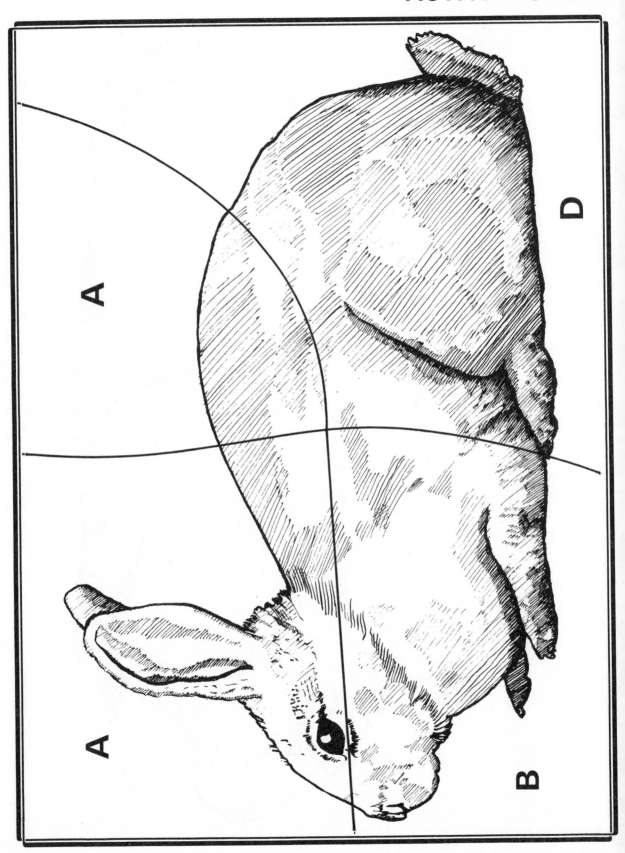

A

A

D

B

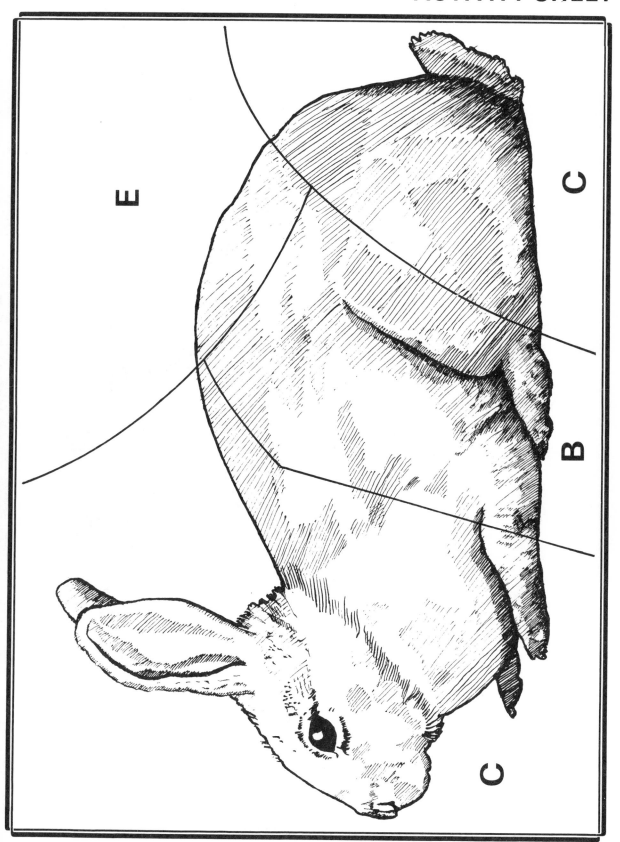

E

C

B

C

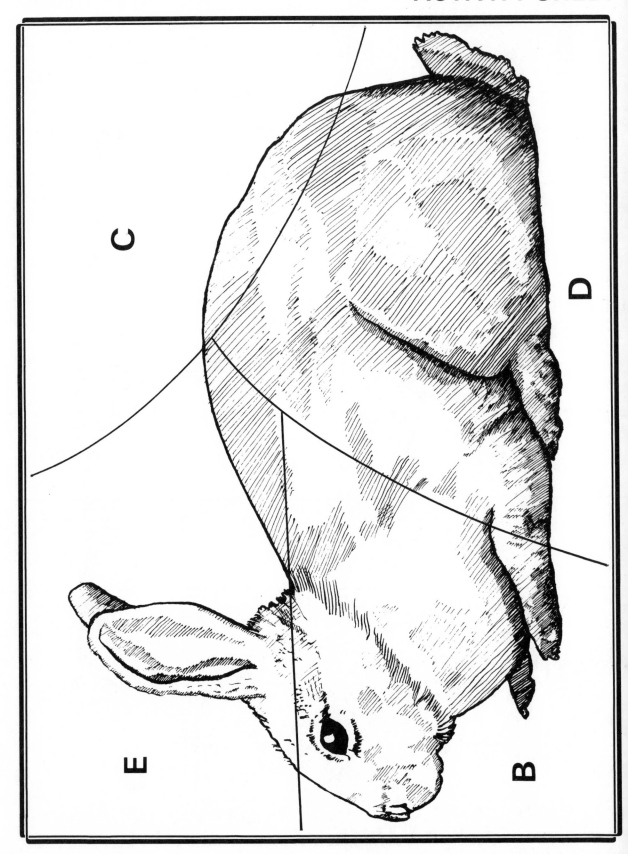

C

D

E

B

1.5   TRUST GAMES

There are various kinds of games which build up trust. Those given here depend on people temporarily giving up their power of sight and having to trust others to look after them. This of course also encourages responsibility and care on the part of those who are leading the 'blind'. However, there needs to be a certain degree of respect and trust among the children before these games can be played safely, so they are not recommended for situations in which respect and trust are at a low ebb.

Leading the blind

The group divides into pairs. One in each pair closes her/his eyes or is blindfolded, while the other is the leader who will guide her/his 'blind' partner. The guidance can be purely physical or it can include verbal instructions. (It is best if you decide whether the leaders should remain silent.) If verbal guidance is included, the leader can start by explaining to the 'blind' partner where she is taking him and what to expect as they walk, and can reassure him that he will not bump into anything. Once trust has been established, she may like to let her partner feel different textures and shapes and perhaps guess what the objects are. After some minutes the partners switch roles. The group can then get together and discuss how it felt to lead and to be led.

Imagined blind journeys

One child leads his/her 'blind' partner across and under chairs, tables, benches and other furniture, describing an imaginary journey as they go. For example, 'Here's an underground passage into the castle . . .' 'Now we must climb over this gate . . .' The journey might be extended into the playground.

Blind encounters

Everyone is 'blind' and they move slowly about the room. When they meet someone else, each gently feels the other's face and perhaps thinks who the other person might be. They then move on. It is best if people keep their eyes closed throughout, rather than looking to see whom they have met. It is the experience of touching each other in this way which is important.

Blind walk

Ask the whole class to stand at one end of the room. In turn, everyone closes their eyes and walks (or runs) the length of the room, while you gently receive and stop them at the other end. If the room is long, the second child should start walking before the first has reached you.

Variation A group of children joins you and they help to receive and stop the rest of the class.

SECTION 2 LOOKING FOR SOLUTIONS TO EVERYDAY CONFLICTS

Everyone is familiar with the conflicts that occur in our day-to-day interaction with others. Sometimes other people do not share our attitudes or opinions, sometimes they do things which prevent us from doing or having what we want. The aim of this section is to develop children's understanding of conflicts that arise in the familiar setting of the school or the home and to help them explore different ways of resolving such conflicts. They are encouraged to look at all the facts presented by each conflict, to try to understand each point of view and to question their own feelings. They can then evaluate the situation in the light of their discoveries. It is important to stress that there are no right or wrong ways of resolving conflicts, only solutions that leave people more or less happy or hurt.

Conflict resolution can best be tackled in an atmosphere which is supportive rather than critical, so that the children do not feel threatened. If they can learn to understand and deal with small-scale conflicts, they should be in a better position to understand the conflicts they see portrayed in the media.

The lesson ideas in this section include a variety of activities such as writing, discussion, drama, games, art and puppetry. Obviously you will want to select the activities that are most suitable for your class.

Lesson ideas for the teacher	Activity sheets for the children
2.1 Introducing the concepts of peace, conflict and violence	
2.2 Starting to look at conflicts	Looking at a conflict Arguments Cartoon Sheets 1, 2, 3 Picture story
2.3 Using drama to explore conflicts between individuals	Drama Sheets 1, 2, 3, 4
2.4 Further drama exercises	Conversations Happenings
2.5 Conflicts between groups	
2.6 A closer look at solutions	
2.7 Conflict scenarios	

Further Resources

T: for the teacher, C: for the children

Donna Brandes and Howard Phillips, *Gamesters' Handbook*, Hutchinson, 1979. (T)

Donna Brandes, *Gamesters' Handbook 2*, Hutchinson, 1982. (T)

Christopher Day, *Drama for Middle and Upper Schools*, Batsford. (T)

Simon Fisher and David Hicks, *World Studies 8–13: A Teacher's Handbook*, Oliver & Boyd, 1985. (T)

Irish Commission for Justice and Peace/Irish Council of Churches, *Free to be*. (T/C)

Mildred Masheder, *Let's Co-operate : Activities and Ideas for Parents and Teachers of Young Children*, Peace Education Project, 1986. (T)

Cecily O'Neill *et al*, *Drama Guidelines*, Heinemann Educational, 1977. (T)

Anna Scher and Charles Verrall, *100+ Ideas for drama*, Heinemann Educational, 1975. (T)

Schools Council Moral Education Project, *Choosing* books especially *Book 1: What shall I do? Book 4: Getting it right*; also *Teacher's Book: Moral education in the middle years*. (T/C)

For books on peace, violence and aggression, see p. 95.

2.1 INTRODUCING THE CONCEPTS OF PEACE, CONFLICT AND VIOLENCE

It is important to begin by establishing how the children understand these concepts. This can be done by having a 'brainstorm'. Write the word 'conflict' on the board and ask the children to think of any word or phrase which they associate with conflict. Write up all the suggestions without comment. Then stop and go through the list trying to code the responses in some way. For example, you could tick those which in the children's opinion involve physical violence and put a star against those which refer to a clash of ideas. The class could then try to agree on a smaller number of responses which together give a good picture of what conflict is, and these could be underlined. Obviously the value of brainstorming lies largely in the thought and discussion which it involves.

When the topic of conflict is exhausted, you could deal with violence and then peace in a similar manner. (See the definitions below.)

Follow-up

Encourage children to talk about their most peaceful and/or violent memory, drawing either from their own experience or from something they have seen or read.

Some children might like to write about and/or illustrate the peaceful or violent experience that they described.

The children could make a collage of violent words and images cut from newspapers and magazines, followed by a collage on the theme of peace. The two could be displayed side by side.

Groups or individuals could design and make a badge that symbolizes peace and/or violence. Their logo could then be used to decorate future work they produce on these themes.

The children could explore the concepts of peace, conflict, and violence by using the picture set (see Introduction: footnote).

Some definitions

Below are some dictionary definitions of the three words which might help you clarify your thoughts.

CONFLICT   1 a struggle, fight or battle
                  2 a clashing of arguments or interests
                  3 a mental struggle within a person

VIOLENCE   1 physical force used to injure people or damage property
                  2 excessive, unrestrained or unjustifiable force

PEACE   1 freedom from war, conflict, activity, noise
                  2 state of quiet, stillness, harmony

In this book 'conflict' is usually used in the second of the senses above, and the children are encouraged to explore ways of preventing a clashing of interests from developing into a fight (or conflict in the first sense).

2.2 STARTING TO LOOK AT CONFLICTS

It is best to start by taking examples of conflicts of the kind that the children in the class have experienced. You could ask them to describe conflicts in which they have recently been involved, or take conflicts which they have already talked about in the follow-up above. Alternatively, you could take a few of the conflict scenarios on pp. 49–50. (If you intend to use the drama and cartoon cards later, you should choose scenarios without crosses or asterisks.) Let the children get into pairs or small groups and consider their chosen conflict with the help of the questions on p. 31 'Looking at a conflict'.

The class could then come together to share their thoughts. As the discussion develops, children who have not contributed may feel inclined to talk about their personal experience of conflict, perhaps as they identify with the examples under discussion. The session could end with an analysis of the most common causes of children's conflicts, such as differences of opinion or attitude, wanting different things, wanting the same thing but not being able or willing to share.

Follow-up

Groups or individuals might like to produce a painting, collage or cartoon that shows the progression of a conflict.

Individuals and/or groups could use the activity sheets:

ARGUMENTS (p. 32) After responding to the questions on the sheet, the children might like to develop their thoughts and produce an illustrated story.

CARTOONS (pp. 33–35) Give cartoon sheets to individuals or small groups and ask 'What happens next?' The answers could be presented as further pictures or as pieces of writing.

PICTURE STORY (p. 36) Copies of this can be given to individuals or pairs. (The picture is taken from a poster designed by Quaker Peace and Service.)

LOOKING AT A CONFLICT

Take a particular conflict, perhaps one in which at least one of you has been involved, and discuss the following questions:

1 Who is involved in the conflict?
2 How did it start?
3 Why has it happened?
4 What does each side/person hope to gain from the conflict?
5 How does each side/person feel?
6 What might happen next?
7 Is there a solution that each side/person would agree to and feel happy with?

ARGUMENTS

Think of an argument that you have had at school or at home that stands out in your mind.

Now imagine that you are being questioned about your part in the argument by either a judge, a policeman or a newspaper reporter.

The questions you will be asked are:
When did this argument take place?
Where were you at that time?
Who else was at the scene of the argument?
How did the argument start?
What is your version of what happened next?
How did the argument end?
Was the problem solved or might it happen again?
Can you think of a better ending to the argument now?

Write down your answers to these questions.

Now imagine you are the other person in your argument and write down the answers you think he/she would give to the same questions!

PICTURE STORY

What is the message of this picture story?
Can you draw or write a story about people which has a similar message?

This page may be photocopied

2.3 USING DRAMA TO EXPLORE CONFLICTS BETWEEN INDIVIDUALS

Dramatising a situation of conflict can help children understand how both sides feel and encourage them to explore different ways of reaching a solution. Four different approaches to the use of drama in developing conflict scenarios are described below, so that you can choose the method most suited to your situation. Conflict scenarios can be taken either from the list on pp. 49–50 or from the children's own suggestions. Alternatively, if the children have just been involved in or witnessed a conflict, that might provide an excellent starting point.

When using drama it is important to remember that some of the best sessions may be somewhat unpredictable, following whatever arises spontaneously. The ideas given here are meant as starting points and guidelines. It is good to begin drama sessions with a few simple games and activities to help the children warm up. You might like to use some of the games in Section 1 for this purpose before starting on the drama exercises given here. Many more games and warm-up activities are to be found in the drama and games books listed on pp. 3–4 and 27–28.

1 Improvising without restrictions

Choose a conflict scenario and let the children divide into pairs or small groups depending on the number of characters required. Describe the situation to the class and let each pair/group decide who is playing which part and where the scene is taking place. The children then immediately start improvising the scene, unprepared and relying fully on their immediate reactions.

Afterwards they can look at the consequences of their actions. We are all aware of thinking after an event 'If only I'd said/done such and such.' The children should be encouraged to discuss how else they might have acted.

How did they feel in each role?
Were some of the feelings unpleasant, hostile, angry?
Could a happier ending be found?
Would that ending please both sides and stop further conflict?

The children should then be encouraged to act out various possible endings to their conflict and to invent extra characters if this will help them to reach a solution. They should also try reversing roles so that they can experience both sides of the argument.

The session could end with each group's final version of the conflict and its solution.

The advantage of this method of using drama to explore conflict resolution is that the children can experience the consequences of their immediate reactions. In this way they may come to realise that violent responses can have negative effects. The discussion following the improvisation is crucial. The disadvantage of this method, of course, is that the children may feel this is the cue for hitting or shouting at each other. In that case, either one pair/group can enact the scene in front of the others, so that you can stop them if they are becoming violent and ask them where their actions are likely to lead, or one of the following methods can be chosen instead.

2 Improvising with restrictions

The procedure is as above, except that the children are told that violence is not permitted. They have to find non-violent solutions to the conflicts.

3 Using Puppets

Some children might be encouraged to enter their roles more freely through the use of puppets. Either of the above improvisation methods may be used with puppets carrying out the actions.

Puppets can be made quite simply from socks or paper bags. In both cases, eyes, mouth and hair can be made from scraps of material and wool and then glued on (or in the case of sock puppets they can also be sewn on). If paper bags are used faces can also be drawn.

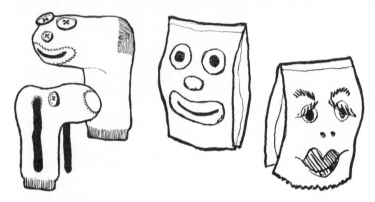

4 Using Drama Sheets

Small groups of children work from drama sheets. Four are included in this section (pp. 39–42). Further sheets can easily be made by substituting other scenarios.

Follow-up

A group or class play could be staged based on one of the conflicts. This would involve activities such as script writing, costume design and the creation of sound effects.

Characters

Bully   Younger Child   Teacher
Plus any extras you need for the ending you invent

SCENE ONE

In the school playground a bully chases and kicks a younger child. The child begins to cry. The bully threatens to beat up the child if the teacher is told about what's happened. The teacher appears on the scene.

WHAT TO DO

1 Imagine the scene. You can add details and include onlookers if you wish. Decide in your group who will act each character. Don't worry if you don't each have a part to play in Scene One as you may need to invent more characters in the next scene.
2 Act out Scene One.
3 Talk in your group about what happens next. Can you find an ending that you all agree would solve the problem? Would each of the characters be happy with the ending you choose?
4 Now act out Scene Two.
5 Try swapping parts with the other actors in your group. Talk about how you felt as each character.

FURTHER IDEAS

Show your play to the class.
Write out your play showing the lines that each character has to say.
Make a puppet for each character and put on a puppet play.

Characters

Five Children   Teacher

Plus any extras you need for the ending you invent

SCENE ONE

On the playing field: One child comes to the teacher saying that she has hurt her leg and cannot run in the race. Four other children ask to be allowed to replace her. The teacher picks the child whom the others regard as the teacher's favourite, even though the other three were faster runners in the practice.

WHAT TO DO

1 Decide in your group who will act each character. Don't worry if you don't each have a part to play in Scene One as you may need to invent more characters in the next scene.
2 Act out Scene One.
3 Talk in your group about what happens next. Can you find an ending that you all agree would solve the problem? Would each of the characters be happy with the ending you choose?
4 Now act out Scene Two.
5 Try swapping parts with the other actors in your group. Talk about how you felt as each character.

FURTHER IDEAS

Show your play to the class.

Write out your play showing the lines that each character has to say.

Make a puppet for each character and put on a puppet play.

Characters

2 groups of three (or more) children
Plus any extras you need for the ending you invent

SCENE ONE

In the classroom: The first group of children decide to sit together and place their books around a table. They then go to fetch their pens. While they are away, the second group of children comes in. They decide they want to sit at the same table, so they throw the first group's books on to the floor and sit down. The first group returns.

WHAT TO DO

1 Decide in your group who will act each character. Don't worry if you don't each have a part to play in Scene One as you may need to invent more characters in the next scene.
2 Act out Scene One.
3 Talk in your group about what happens next. Can you find an ending that you all agree would solve the problem? Would each of the characters be happy with the ending you choose?
4 Now act out Scene Two.
5 Try swapping parts with the other actors in your group. Talk about how you felt as each character.

FURTHER IDEAS

Show your play to the class.
Write out your play showing the lines that each character has to say.
Make a puppet for each character and put on a puppet play.

Characters
Three children
Plus any extras you need for the ending you invent

SCENE ONE
In the living room: Three children are watching the television. Suddenly one jumps up half-way through the programme and turns to another channel to watch a serial she is following. The other two want to continue watching their programme.

WHAT TO DO
1 Decide in your group who will act each character. Don't worry if you don't each have a part to play in Scene One as you may need to invent more characters in the next scene.
2 Act out Scene One.
3 Talk in your group about what happens next. Can you find an ending that you all agree would solve the problem? Would each of the characters be happy with the ending you choose?
4 Now act out Scene Two.
5 Try swapping parts with the other actors in your group. Talk about how you felt as each character.

FURTHER IDEAS
Show your play to the class.
Write out your play showing the lines that each character has to say.
Make a puppet for each character and put on a puppet play.

2.4 FURTHER DRAMA EXERCISES

These provide opportunities to explore different possible responses to a variety of conflict situations. They are divided into 'Conversations' and 'Happenings'.

Conversations

The children divide into pairs. Each pair has to decide who is A and who is B. The pair is then given one of the conversation extracts on p. 44. The children have to devise a situation in which those words are likely to appear. (They do not have to use the exact words so long as the meaning remains.) Alternatively, they can design a scene which begins or ends with the words, or two different scenes which both share that snippet of conversation.

Happenings

These are best used in small groups. They can be introduced in two ways:

1 Set the scene for the happening by explaining the characters, activity, location and time, and leading the group to develop this general situation. Then introduce the happening, either by doing it or by announcing it, depending on what it is. Explain to the children beforehand that there is going to be a happening and they must react to it in role.

2 Let the children divide into groups and describe a happening to each group. These happenings are to be the starting points for improvisations.

Some examples of happenings are given on p. 45. In the first five, only the bare bones of the happening are given, leaving you and the children to create the situation. In the others the situation is sketched in outline because it is essential to the happening.

CONVERSATIONS

These can be photocopied and cut up to give to the children

At Home

1. A Can I go out now?
   B Not till you've completely finished.

2. A Who said you could take that?
   B No-one.
   A Put it back then.

3. A Why do you always have to be different from other people? Answer me that!

At School

1. A I'm not going to tell him.
   B Well I'm not.

2. A You wanted to see me?
   B Yes, I want a word with you.

3. A Leave him alone, can't you?
   B He started it!

4. A Go on, don't be a coward!
   B Alright, are you coming?
   A If you are.

5. A Alright, own up, who was it?

Open Situations The children decide who, where, when and what it's all about.

1. A What are you doing with that?
   B I was only only borrowing it.

2. A 'Ere, you haven't paid.
   B Yes I have.
   A I don't give free rides.
   B I've paid, I tell you!

3. A How much longer do I have to wait?
   B I don't know.
   A DON'T KNOW?!

4. A Anything to declare?
   B Please, I'm in a hurry.
   A Anything to declare?
   B No.
   A Just open that bag.
   B That one! Oh, alright.
   A What's this, sir?

HAPPENINGS

These can be photcopied and cut up to give to the children.

At School

1 Fire alarm goes.

2 A and B are to see the Headmaster at once.

3 Loud crash and sound of yelling.

At Home

4 There is a furious banging at the front door.

5 There is a loud bang followed by a scream.

6 You're in your room. It's late. There's a noise downstairs. You thought you were alone in the house.

In the Factory

7 Several false fire alarms recently. Productivity has fallen and affected bonuses. Everyone's working flat out to make up for lost time. Fire alarm goes off. Everyone has to evacuate by the rules.

8 A mate is sacked. He's already been picked on quite often by the foreman. The reason given for the sacking was lateness. His wife's in hospital and he is having to see the children off to school. As a union member, you think it's unfair.

Open Situations

9 You are sitting in an airport. The man sitting next to you has his suitcase open. You think you can see the barrel of a gun.

10 Someone pushes your arm and takes something from you. You catch him up as he jumps into a lift. You are both alone as the doors close.

11 A rather badly smelling drunk lurches towards you and insists you lend him some money. As you walk away he follows you.

2.5 CONFLICTS BETWEEN GROUPS

Most of the conflicts considered so far have been between individuals and have not involved the interests of groups or communities. It is important to help children relate interpersonal conflicts to those in the wider world and again this can be achieved through drama. An example of a drama session which leads into a community conflict is given here.

Zoo or Airport? – A conflict between groups

1 Introduce the idea of various relationships involving animals by using the drama game 'Strike a pose'. Ask the children, in pairs, to create a series of quick poses. These could include 'man/woman and dog', 'cat and mouse', 'hunter and lion' and 'zookeeper and elephant'. Each pose should be created immediately, without discussion.

2 Tell the children that they are all animals at the zoo. Help them to get into role by asking questions such as: What kind of animal are you? What is your cage or enclosure like? What are you doing? Are you enjoying yourself?

3 Now change the scene and tell the children that they are all at an airport. Help them by asking questions such as: Who are you – a passenger, a pilot, a steward or stewardess, a mechanic? What are you doing? What do you see around you? What are you feeling?

4 After this, explain that there is an area of land outside the town where they live and there are two proposals for its use: as a zoo and as a local airport. Let them divide into pairs, X and Y, for four short role plays:

a) X is a journalist interviewing Y, who is manager of the proposed zoo, about why the zoo should be created.

b) Y is a journalist interviewing the co-ordinator of the local Animal Rights group about why they think the zoo should not be allowed.

c) Y is again the journalist, this time interviewing the manager of the proposed airport about how it might benefit the area.

d) X is a journalist interviewing the co-ordinator of the Residents' Association which represents the people living next to the proposed site. X wants to know why the residents are against having an airport on their doorstep.

5 Divide the class arbitrarily into four equal-sized groups:

the people who would run the zoo

the people who would run the airport

the local Animal Rights group

the Residents' Association for the area adjoining the proposed site

Each group is going to send a representative to a public meeting which will decide what the site should be used for. Let the groups first discuss the arguments they wish to put forward, letting everyone have their say. You may want to circulate among the groups and help the discussions along with questions or suggestions. Then ask each group to choose their representative.

6 The scene now moves to the public meeting. A chairperson will be needed (either you or one of the children). Any child without a special role is a member of the public. The representatives should each be given a few minutes to put forward their cases, after which the public may submit questions or comments. A vote is then taken.

7 The class should now come together for discussion:

How were the representatives chosen? Did the groups vote?

Did the groups feel that their representatives gave a fair summary of their views?

How did the representatives feel on this matter?

Did the representatives experience a conflict between saying what they themselves felt and putting forward the views of their group?

In what kinds of situation do people choose representatives? How are they chosen?

Further drama activities

Drama can also be used to explore other conflicts between groups over issues such as use of land or other resources. For example, you could set the scene for a debate about the proposed construction of a bypass. Groups involved might include people living in the path of the proposed bypass, people living on busy town centre roads, lorry drivers, pedestrians, shop-keepers and Friends of the Earth. Or the conflict might be over whether a sum of money should be spent on a new community centre or on an adventure playground.

Follow-up

Discuss how the idea of small groups electing representatives relates to that of parliamentary democracy. Approximately how many people do the local Members of Parliament represent? How can people make their views known to their MP?

2.6   A CLOSER LOOK AT SOLUTIONS

This allows the children to examine the ways in which they have been solving their improvised conflicts and introduces a link with conflict resolution in a wider context.

The class makes a list of the different ways in which the improvised conflicts were settled. All suggestions are recorded and four basic methods may well become apparent:

Aggression
Withdrawal
Discussion and negotiation
Decision by a third party

The advantages and disadvantages of such methods should then be discussed.

Follow-up

The four methods could be discussed in relation to national and international conflicts that the children have heard about, such as strikes, trade union disputes, government debates, civil unrest, wars and cold wars. A consideration of the use of a third party to solve disputes could lead to a study of the role of the United Nations.

A Peace Hero or Heroine could be invented whose task is to solve conflicts wherever they arise.

The activities in this section could be related to the 'World Garden' idea in Section 8 (p. 152).

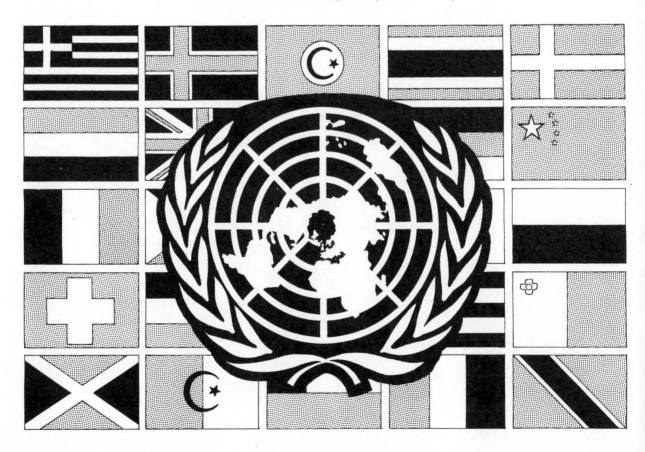

2.7 CONFLICT SCENARIOS

Below are some examples of children's conflicts.

Scenarios marked with an asterisk *are used in the drama sheets.
Those marked with a cross + are used in the cartoon sheets.

Between children

In a classroom one child deliberately spoils another child's work but refuses to own up when questioned by the teacher.

* In the playground a bully chases and kicks a younger child but threatens to beat the child up after school if the teacher finds out.

+ Two children are playing with a ball in the playground when a third child asks to join in. The first child agrees but the second child does not like the newcomer and says no.

A child finds that his pen is missing. He sees another child with an identical pen and accuses her of stealing it. That child says that she brought the pen from home.

A playful child hides a friend's new rubber and refuses to give it back. A third child knows where the rubber is but is afraid that the playful child will seek revenge if she intervenes.

The class is lining up for dinner when the teacher asks the first child to throw some litter into the bin. The other children refuse to allow the child back to the front of the line.

Something very valuable goes missing from a child's desk. She is fairly sure who took it. She is talking to (i) a friend (ii) the teacher (iii) the suspect. (Various explanations can be suggested eg that the friend borrowed it and broke it, or else the child misplaced it and it's in the cloakroom.)

Between teacher and child

+ Paint has been spilt over a child's work. The teacher blames that child but the other children working from the same paint pot know that it was not that child's fault. The children know which one of them was responsible for spilling the paint.

Two children are always scoring the same results in class tests. The teacher accuses the weaker child of cheating but both deny the charge.

* Four children want to be chosen to replace an injured runner in a school race. The teacher picks a child whom the others regard as the teacher's favourite, even though the other three were faster runners in the practice.

A piece of school equipment is accidentally broken. The teacher asks for the person responsible to own up and, when no-one does, threatens to keep the whole class behind after school.

A child accidentally breaks a window. It's not really his fault, but he has been in a lot of trouble recently and doesn't want to own up. He is talking to (i) the caretaker (ii) a teacher (iii) a friend.

Between one group and another

* A group of children decide to sit together and place their books around a table. They then go to fetch their pens. When they return their books have been thrown on the floor and another group of children has taken their seats.

A gang of children are returning home after school when they see a smaller group of children from a neighbouring school. They threaten the smaller group and seem to be looking for a fight.

+ Two groups of rival supporters need to take the same train home after the match. The supporters of the winning side tease the losers and insult their team. The supporters of the losing team feel that the referee was biased and that their team should have won.

Between members of a family

Granny is coming to stay for a fortnight. There is no spare bedroom, so Mum asks one child to give up her own bedroom. She refuses.

A child has been collecting cards and nearly has a complete set. His brother (or sister) gives one away to a friend who needs it. The child is furious when he finds out that the card is missing.

* Three children are watching the television when one jumps up half-way through the programme and turns to another channel to watch a serial she is following. The other two want to continue watching their programme, and protest.

Two children share a bedroom. One is reading when the other bursts in noisily and begins to practise his drumming. He has to play in the bedroom as the rest of the family cannot bear the noise. The first child protests at being disturbed.

A child goes to the rescue of a smaller child who is being bullied. This leads to a fight in which the children's clothes get badly torn, and their faces scratched. The bully runs off leaving both children to explain to their angry parents how they got themselves into such a mess.

A child requests more pocket money, and the parent refuses.

A child comes in late from a disco and is told off by worried parents. She says she couldn't help being late, but her parents threaten not to let her go out again for a month.

The parent(s) decide that the children should help more about the house, starting today. But today is the big match (or they have made other plans) and beg to be allowed to postpone helping till tomorrow.

Public situations
(*more suitable for older children.*)

You leave your bike outside a shop. When you return, it's gone. Later you see someone pushing an identical bike.

You are late for a train, you have the money to pay for the ticket but if you queue for a ticket you will miss the train. It's the last one. The ticket officer on the gate, going by the book, insists on you having a ticket and won't take your money.

Someone has nipped into the car parking space you were just about to back into. You start to argue, but the other driver doesn't understand you. He speaks another language.

PART B WIDER WORLD

The first part of the book looked at conflict within the child's immediate experience. This part considers conflict and violence that children experience at second hand, through the media. It aims to provide a bridge between the child's small world and global issues, and to help the child realise that the media have to select what to present and how to present it, and thus their picture of the world is a constructed one.

SECTION 3 LOOKING AT THE WORLD THROUGH NEWSPAPERS

This section aims to show that news can be presented in different ways and that newspapers, like all the media, are inevitably selective in what they communicate. It also helps children to become familiar with newspapers and to understand how they are produced. It includes some consideration of newspaper coverage of conflict and violence. Some of the activities in this section require the children to read and understand newspaper articles, which means that these are suitable only for older or more able children .

Lesson ideas for the teacher	Activity sheets for the children
3.1 Activities using a collection of different papers	What gets reported Conflicts portrayed in the papers
3.2 Looking at bias	
3.3 Further experience with newspapers	Looking at advertisements

Further Resources

T: for the teacher, C: for the children

Sarah Allen, *Making a Newspaper*, Cambridge University Press, 1984. (C)

Floyd L Bergman, *The English Teacher's Activities Handbook – An Ideabook for Middle and Secondary Schools*, Allyn and Bacon, 1982. (T)

Andrew Bethell, *Viewpoint*, Cambridge University Press, 1979. (T/C)

Ross Davies, *Inside Fleet Street*, Priory Press, 1976. (C)

L R Green and H M Sawyer, *Write Your Own Newspaper*, Macmillan Educational, 1985. (C)

Derek Heater, *World Studies: Education for International Understanding in Britain*, Harrap, 1980 – Ch. 5 'The Teacher and the Media'. (T)

Penny Junor, *Newspaper*, Macdonald Educational, 1979. (C)

Andrew Langley, *Newspaper*, Franklin Watts, 1985. (C)

Colin Reid (ed), *Issues in Peace Education*, D Brown & Sons, 1984 – Richard Keeble, 'Media Images of Violence and Peace'. (T)

Schools Council/Rowntree Project, *World Studies 8–13: Some Classroom Activities – Interim Paper 3*, Schools Council Publications, 1982.* (T)

*The author gratefully acknowledges permission to use some ideas from this paper in the present chapter.

3.1 ACTIVITIES USING A COLLECTION OF DIFFERENT PAPERS

You need to bring in a selection of daily papers, both national and local. All should be of the same date. Let the class divide into small groups and give each group a newspaper. Try and ensure that groups which are given large and wordy papers contain at least one good reader.

It is best to start by letting each group familiarize itself with its paper by trying to find out how the contents are arranged.

Where is the sports news? The weather forecast? The letters page? Are there cartoons? Crosswords?

Before embarking on the activities, you will also need to ask questions such as:
What does an editor do?
What is an editorial? An article? A headline?
What does 'readership' mean?
What counts as 'news' and what does not?

Some or all of the following five activities can then be undertaken.

1 Ask each group to read out the main headlines on the front page of their newspaper.

What do the various headlines mean?
How do they differ?
Do the headlines tell us anything about the paper and its readership?
Whereabouts does the news item that makes the headlines in one paper appear in other papers?
Look at the words used in the headlines. What do these words have in common? (For instance, how long are they? How many are aggressive or violent?)

Ask the class to suggest other ways in which papers differ. The children might think of things like the size of the pages, the thickness of the newspaper, the size of the headlines and the amount of space devoted to text, to pictures and to advertisements.

2 Choose a news item which appears in all the papers and ask each group to cut the item out. All the cuttings should be mounted on a large sheet of paper with the name of the newspaper beneath each article and a note of which page it was on. When all the children have had a chance to read the articles, encourage them to discuss the differences:

How do the articles differ?

What has each article left out?

Why do you think the articles differ?

Do you think that some or all of the newspapers are biased?

Can you be sure that you are not biased when you try to answer this question?

Is it ever possible to produce a true and complete account of what happened?

This should lead on to the question of where the papers get their news from and how they select what to feature (see pp. 60 and 61).

3 Discussion exercises can be used to encourage the children to consider what kind of picture of the world a newspaper gives. Such exercises are also valuable in that they present a group with the task of reaching agreement.

Owen coalition terms upset Labour

By NICK ASSINDER
Political Reporter

A MANIFESTO for a Tory-Alliance coalition after the next election was mapped out by SDP leader David Owen yesterday.

His blueprint led furious Labour MPs to accuse him of showing his 'true-blue' colours and planning to keep Mrs Thatcher in Downing Street.

It also angered some Liberals, who fear they are about to be 'stitched up' by Dr

Owen and who feel they have more in common with Labour.

Labour's campaign co-ordinator Bryan Gould said: 'Dr Owen has come out in his true-blue colours. He almost revealed his ready-packaged terms for a post-election deal with Mrs Thatcher.

'This comes as no surprise to

the Labour Party. We have known for months that he is hell-bent on keeping Labour out of office. But it will surprise and alarm many Liberals. Anyone who thinks a vote for the Alliance is a means of getting rid of Mrs Thatcher will discover that in

Turn to Page 2, Col 6

Owen admits problems over electoral reform

By Anthony Bevins
Political Editor

THE ALLIANCE would be powerless to impose proportional representation on a minority Government, even if the Conservatives or Labour accepted otherwise tough terms for a coalition over two to three years, David Owen conceded yesterday.

"This is practical reality," the Social Democratic Party leader said in an interview on London Weekend Television's *Weekend World*.

"You know how difficult it is to get constitutional issues through the House of Commons anyhow. If you are trying to dragoon people who don't believe in it, you are in very great difficulty."

Dr Owen's remarks will cause disappointment in the Liberal wing of the Alliance. Even the recent joint policy statement, *The Time has Come*, said proportional representation would be "a crucial priority" in negotiations with a minority Government.

But Dr Owen said yesterday that, while electoral reform might be expected for the European Parliament, a Scottish assembly and even local government, PR for Westminster was different.

"Your problem is always that MPs are free men and women. I believe that, and the Alliance believes that," he said. "You can't expect free men and women to suspend all their judgement. If they think it's bad, if they think it's wrong, they won't vote for it.

"And in many ways I think they are right to do that. I don't want a Parliament which is capable of making really fundamental changes on the basis of what they don't believe, purely and simply to cling to office. So we have a dilemma.

"The question that we have to face ourselves is how much are they defending vested interests, and how much are they taking account of the views of the country."

Dr Owen said he sympathised with the view that the issue should be put to the country in a special referendum after a coalition deal had been struck with a minority Government.

He repeated that the Alliance

would vote down any Queen's Speech programme which had not previously been agreed. As far as co-operation with the Conservatives was concerned, Mrs Thatcher would be required to change her economic policies to produce a fall in unemployment, Dr Owen said.

But he appeared to relax the Alliance demand for the cancellation of the Trident replacement for Polaris, saying that it would be sufficient for the Conservatives to consider an alternative like the French M5 missile system, or submarine-launched cruise.

Dr Owen insisted, however, that while Labour's heart was in the right place on unemployment, Neil Kinnock would have to concede a continuation of Polaris patrols if he wanted Alliance support, and there could be no question of a repeal of Conservative legislation on trade union reform.

"He has got to change his views on nuclear policy and defence," Dr Owen said. "There is no question of that. So has Mrs Thatcher got to change her policies on unemployment."

Row looming over Owen's terms for pact with Tories

Ban-the-bomb Labour is snubbed

ASTONISHING terms by Dr David Owen for a Coalition Government with the Tories were rocking the Alliance last night.

The leader of the Social Democrats laid down the rules for a pact with Mrs Thatcher, if there is a hung Parliament.

He ruled out a deal with Labour—unless it ditches its ban-the-bomb policies.

But he indicated the Alliance would back Trident nuclear submarines, as long as Tory leaders agreed to look for cheaper missiles to put in them.

His terms for a Tory-Alliance link-up

By PAUL WILENIUS
Home Affairs Correspondent

look certain to spark a Liberal backlash. Many rank-and-file Liberals are still bitter about the deal worked out with the SDP on nuclear weapons.

Last September the Liberals voted at their national conference to go for a non-nuclear defence policy. But a deal was patched up by Alliance leaders.

Dr Owen's apparent wooing of the Tories, especially over nuclear weapons, will alarm Liberals keen to get rid of the bomb. The SDP leader also said he would refuse to do a deal with Labour if it insisted on getting rid of all the Tory trade union reforms.

Labour would find it extremely hard to abandon its policy of scrapping nuclear weapons and not to reverse the union laws.

Surprise

Labour campaign co-ordinator Bryan Gould said after Dr Owen outlined his coalition terms on ITV's Weekend World that a vote for the Alliance was a vote for the Tories.

He said: "Dr Owen came out in his true-blue colours.

"He also revealed his ready-package terms for a post-election deal with Mrs Thatcher.

"We have known for months that he is hell bent on keeping Labour out of office. But it will surprise and alarm many Liberals.

"Anyone who thinks a vote for the Alliance is a means of getting rid of Mrs Thatcher will discover that in Dr Owen's hands, their vote will keep her in Downing Street."

TERMS: Dr Owen

Owen's 'true blue colours'

By DAVID BRADSHAW

SDP leader David Owen gave a clear hint yesterday that in a hung parliament he would rather form a coalition government with the Tories than with Labour.

Virtually slamming the door on any deal with Labour leader Neil Kinnock Dr Owen said on ITV's Weekend World: "The gap between the Alliance and the Conservatives is not unbridgeable."

Bryan Gould, Labour's campaign co-ordinator, said: "He has come out in his true blue colours."

Owen 'rules out' pact on government with Labour

By Richard Evans, Political Correspondent

Dr David Owen was accused last night by Labour's campaign co-ordinator of being hellbent on keeping Labour out of office in the event of a hung Parliament.

The outburst by Mr Bryan Gould came after the SDP leader roundly confined his criticism of the Government to Mrs Margaret Thatcher and emphasized that there were large numbers of Conservative MPs who favoured a change in economic policy and were not committed to Trident which would make a deal with the Alliance much easier.

In contrast, he attacked the "loony left" within Labour's ranks, the leadership of Mr Neil Kinnock and pointed to major sticking points involving the repeal of trade union legislation and the abandonment of Britain's independent nuclear deterrent, which would block any chance of a pact between Labour and the Alliance.

When it was suggested to Dr Owen, who was appearing on *Weekend World* that he had given the clear impression that he was a politician more likely to be able to do a deal with the current Conservative Party than with the current Labour Party the SDP leader simply replied: "Well that's up to Mr Kinnock."

Mr Gould said last night: "Dr Owen came out in his true blue colours. He almost revealed his ready packaged terms for a post-election deal with Mrs Thatcher. "Anyone who thinks a vote for the Alliance is a means of getting

rid of Mrs Thatcher will discover that in Dr Owen's hands their vote will simply keep her in Downing Street."

Dr Owen, speaking about Alliance priorities in the event of no overall general election victory, disclosed he now favoured a referendum on proportional representation for Westminster elections and suggested it should take place after the legislation had been passed by Parliament "so people know what they're voting for".

In the short term "immediate demands" included the introduction of PR for elections to the European parliament, the proposed legislative parliament for Scotland and a revived Northern Ireland assembly.

While a "very, very big gap" remained between the attitude of Mrs Thatcher and the two Alliance leaders on the economy and unemployment, Dr Owen emphasized that there were a sizeable number of Cabinet ministers and a very substantial number of Conservative MPs who had consistently wanted substantial changes to economic policies. The gap between the Alliance and Conservative parties was not unbridgeable.

And on the key issue of Trident he said there was room for a Conservative Party, which had fought the election backing Trident, "to come round to the view ... that there is another way which is less expensive, not quite so supersophisticated but nevertheless sufficient for British purposes".

If the children have undertaken the two activities described above, they might like to exchange newspapers at this point so that each group has a fresh paper. Ask each group to make a collection of ten cuttings which in their opinion show what life is like in present-day Britain. They must then rank them according to particular criteria. For instance, you could say:

You are writing to a penfriend in Hungary. Which of these cuttings would you think it most important to enclose to show what life in Britain is like?

or,

You are going to bury these cuttings in a time-proof container which will be opened in 100 years time. Which six would you include to show our descendants what life is like now?

When all the groups have made their selections, they should display them on large sheets of paper. The children could then discuss the differences between the displays, using the questions on p. 58 'What gets reported'.

4 When the children have done one or more of the above exercises, ask them to look for articles which are concerned with peace or with violence (or both). They should cut out the articles and then imagine (or draw) a line with PEACE at one end and VIOLENCE at the other. Ask them to place each cutting along the line according to how peaceful or violent they feel it to be. This should lead to discussion of where to put articles which are about both violence and peace, for instance an article about a peacekeeping force. There are of course no right answers. The purpose of the exercise is to encourage the children to think more about the meanings of 'peace' and 'violence', and to see how peace and violence are portrayed in the papers.

5 Ask the children for suggestions of the kinds of conflicts they would expect to find reported in the papers. Encourage them to think about political and trade union disputes, for example, as well as armed conflicts. Then give each group a copy of the activity sheet 'Conflicts portrayed in the papers' (p. 59). The children may well need help with answering some of the questions.

WHAT GETS REPORTED

When you have looked at the display of cuttings showing what life in present-day Britain is like, try to answer the questions below:

1 *Did your group have difficulty in finding the kinds of articles you wanted?*

2 *Do you feel that some displays give a more truthful picture of life in present-day Britain than others? If yes, is this difference related to the kind of papers from which they were drawn? For instance, do local papers give a different picture from national papers?*

3 *How do you think the editor decides what to put in the paper?*

4 *What kinds of news or other articles do you most like to read? Why?*

5 *What kinds of events never get reported in the newspaper? Why do you think this is?*

6 *How do papers differ? For example, do some contain more personal stories and others more political news?*

JACKIE'S FABULOUS BIKE

Jackie Davidson (11) didn't imagine that Christmas could have been as wonderful as it turned out to be!

Only in her wildest dreams did she ever believe that she would get a bike. She got one, and WHAT A BIKE! Said an ecstatic Jackie, "I am over the Moon. It's the best present I've ever had."

Jackie's bike is the latest thing in bike technology. It has an ultra-lightweight, but exceptionally strong, alloy frame, alloy wheels, specially designed axles with the latest advanced bearings and a gearing system developed from research carried out during the Tour de France. Extras include theft-proof lights, saddle bag, wing mirrors and an electronic bell.

A spokesman for the manufacturers said that his company had produced a bike that was lightweight, fast, safe and required very little maintenance because of the advanced technology involved.

Many happy hours of cycling Jackie.

CLASS 1 FIRST CLASS!

Class 1 - 3   Class 2 - 2

A dazzling piece of football wizardry by Dean Richards five minutes from the end of an exciting game against class 2 won this epic struggle for Class 1.

There seemed to be no danger when, in the 85th minute, Dean intercepted a pass deep in his own half. Although he appeared to be well marked, he cleverly beat two opponents then set off down the field. A beautiful body swerve sent the two covering defenders the wrong way, and with only the goalkeeper to beat, he coolly waited until he came off his line and cheekily chipped the ball over his head.

The match was an exciting spectacle from the first whistle. Both sides had obviously come out with the idea of playing attacking football. Class 2 took the lead in the 21st minute with a lovely goal by John Edgely who dribbled past two defenders before placing the ball past Stevens.

This set-back spurred Class 1 on to greater effort and they virtually camped in their opponents' penalty area. After several close things, Richards eventually equalised with a simple tap-in after a mix-up in 2's defence.

In the second half, the pace and excitement didn't slacken. Class 1 took the lead in the 64th minute through Davidson, who scored with a free-kick of such tremendous power that it is doubtful if Baines in the Class 2 goal actually saw the ball. Class 2 equalised in the 80th minute through Johnson. Fisher, on the wing, forced a corner, and from the resulting cross, Johnson rose above 1's defence to power in an unstoppable header.

CONFLICTS PORTRAYED IN THE PAPERS

Find two or three articles about conflicts which have not yet been settled and read them carefully. Then, for each conflict, try to answer the following questions:

1 *Who is involved in the conflict?*
2 *What does each side want?*
3 *How are they trying to get what they want?*
4 *Is either side likely to succeed in getting what it wants? Or do you think both sides will have to compromise?*
5 *How do you think each side is feeling?*
6 *What do you think is the worst thing that might happen? And the best?*

The polite protest for women's rights

BARONESS PLATT of Writtle utters the word feminism with some distaste: it smacks a little too much of extremism for a chairman of the Equal Opportunities Commission.

On the other hand, "equal opportunities" trills happily off her tongue: it has a more healthy ring to it.

"Some of the extreme opinions do undermine our work. Here we don't believe in being extreme or outrageous, it is our duty to promote equal opportunities and uphold the law", she says, whipping a copy of the Sex Discrimination Act out of her handbag and flourishing it. "I always carry it with me."

Since it was set up in 1976, the Equal Opportunities Commission has been constantly criticised for not being extreme enough, for opting for ladylike compromise instead of brutal confrontation.

Under the Act, the commission has two purposes: to eliminate discrimination and to promote equality of opportunity. It has preferred to do the latter and has shied away from the former.

By failing to go on the attack, the critics say, the commission and its message have been marginalised.

Out of government sight in Manchester, the commission is struggling to stay afloat on a £3.4m budget. Since 1976 it has been slowly starved of funds and squeezed of confidence.

Even Baroness Platt has discovered that flourishing the Act is no longer enough to promote the cause. She more m friends.

The ma the failure use its po ment.

A REPORT from the Equal Opportunities Commission, to be published today, raises serious questions about the workings of the Sex Discrimination and Equal Pay Acts.

The report, *Pyrrhic Victories*, by Alice Leonard, finds that after nearly 11 years in operation, the impact of legal action under the legislation has been limited.

It finds widespread evidence of delays in the courts, obstruction by employers and victimisation of those claiming discrimination. At the same time, the commission itself is being accused by experts outside of failing in its job. Its effectiveness as a law enforcement body is in question.

The commission is having to make big cuts and is calling for an urgent injection of cash. It wants to set up new regional offices. But many believe the commission itself is need of a major overhaul; that its procedures need to be simplified, its profile lifted and given new government commitment, particularly in the field of employment.

The Manchester EOC has always been strong on research, education and funding of voluntary bodies — until the cuts. It has actively supported and funded cases brought through the courts by individuals and has had well-publicised success, particularly in Europe.

But it has always been wary of using its real clout: the power of formal investigation.

The EOC is the only body in the country empowered to launch formal investigations into mass discrimination; yet it has used the power only nine times in 11 years.

In several cases no formal com

has been exploited by employers, loath to reform; and by the British courts, loath to adapt to give equal opportunities cases a fair chance; and by trade unions, who are too often loath to commit adequate support.

"It is impossible to reform discriminatory practice by depending on on individual cases alone. The effective use of formal investigations is the only way to secure major change, " he said.

The EOC commissioners argue strongly in favour of achieving quiet co-operation. For a start, it is cheaper. One formal investigation can cost up to £250,000 from

The latest statistics show that women have failed to move up the pay ladder since the Sex Discrimination Act set up the commission in 1976. Then, womens' average earnings were 75.1 per cent of men's — but by 1985, they had fallen to 74 per cent.

Figures show that there are still far higher proportions of men than women in better paid grades. For example, in the civil service 74.9 per cent of clerical assistants are women while 2.6 per cent of permanent secretaries and 1.4 per cent of deputy secretaries are women. In 1985, women made up only 10.2 per cent of general management, but held 73.7 per cent of the jobs in clerical or other related work.

Sarah Helm interviews Lady Platt (right), chairman of the commission, and David McKittrick reports on the success of the Equal Opportunities Commission for Northern Ireland in winning the respect of both employers and unions despite its tiny budget.

and attracting publicity. "It is no good antagonising those with whom we are working," Lady Platt said. We must change attitudes, particularly among older men."

A leading lawyer in the field described this as a sop. "It allows everything to be covered up without exposing the issues. Pick almost any large company, look at its equal opportunities record and you wouldn't have a case for a formal investigation."

The EOC's style is stamped upon it by its strategy-making commissioners, selected by the Home Office

commissioners are allowed to interfere with EOC strategy.

But the commission has recently failed to support contract compliance, seen by many as the most powerful weapon available to campaigners against discrimination. It is a practice already widespread in the United States

Historic towns under pressure

By Tony Aldous

THE PEOPLE who try to manage Britain's historic towns are worried about all sorts of pressures which undermine their efforts — traffic and parking; shopping developments; unsuitable shop fronts; county surveyors who put stone or brick; and, not least, lack of good conservation officers.

These worries emerged at two conferences held in neighbouring cities last week: the Association of Conservation Officers' annual conference in Bristol, and a seminar in Bath on "the management of historic towns".

There are two worrying aspects of shopping development — in-town schemes which damage the

piece, Royal Crescent, loudspeakers regaling residents with accounts of their own history, marring both view and atmosphere.

The highway authority, Avon County, then banned coaches from Royal Crescent, but this produced an outcry from residents of a neighbouring set piece, The Circus, fearful of receiving what the Crescent had rejected.

There was also the problem of 45ft-long articulated lorries manoeuvring to penetrate mediaeval streets. A decade ago, Chichester looked at a Dutch means of keeping big lorries from the centre, [...]ns-shipment de-[...] it attractive but [...]w retailers' de-[...]n-store space for [...]hanging this.

[...]. Lancaster's ar-[...]said his city had [...]l local entrepre-[...]go into partner-[...]run an edge-of-[...]But there were [...]ith less storage [...]s for lorry access [...]e streets needed [...] for shoppers.

[...]on of Conserva-[...]onference drew [...]ites from more [...]uthorities from [...]on. Conservation [...]ey were over-[...]nderpaid. Their [...]vorried that they [...]t candidates of

[...]he Bath seminar [...]) included chief [...]lanners, city en-[...]bers concerned

Tutu to defy Pretoria on detainees

From Tony Allen-Mills
in Johannesburg

THE SOUTH African Government's latest restrictions on political protest will be directly challenged today by Desmond Tutu, the Nobel prize-winner and Archbishop of Cape Town.

The Archbishop intends to hold a lunch-time meeting at St George's Cathedral in Cape Town to pray for the release of detainees held under state of emergency laws. The meeting appears to contravene a new clampdown by Pretoria on any form of expression of support for the release of political detainees.

The curbs were announced on Friday night and provoked strong protests over the weekend. Beyers

Naude, the head of the South African Council of Churches, said the restrictions had moved South Africa "closer to dictatorship".

Helen Suzman, the Progressive Federal Party's spokeswoman on law and order, said she had no intention of being silenced on detention without trial.

Archbishop Tutu told Reuters: "They are virtually saying that we can't even have church services in which we pray for the release of detainees, and that's intolerable."

As with other recent government assaults on its critics, the restrictions are minute in detail and sweeping in scope. They prohibit any expression of support for the release of detainees. It is now illegal to wear a T-shirt demanding that child prisoners be freed, or to sign a petition urging the Government to release detainees. And it is no longer permissible to perform any act as a token of solidarity with or in honour of detainees: thus a church service offering prayers might be illegal.

Pretoria has long been irritated by the efforts of the Detainee Parents Support Committee and other groups to publicise detention without trial. Irritation

turned to anger when the Johannesburg *Star* newspaper repulsed a police attempt to confiscate an issue advertising "National Detainees Day" last month.

The security forces have also been angered by a steady flow of allegations that detainees are systematically tortured or abused.

■ Johannesburg (UPI) — White school heads are studying security proposals calling for the arming of selected teachers. The pro-Government *Rapport* newspaper reported yesterday that the principals had been sent copies of a secret Government memorandum which calls for the arming of selected teachers.

several counts. Les Sparks, Bath's director of environmental services, told of the effect of tourist coaches parading slowly past the city's greatest architectural set

with overall town management — decided to establish a contact group to keep each other informed of common problems and possible solutions.

3.2 LOOKING AT BIAS

One way of helping children understand that news is bound to be selective is to let them watch a television news bulletin (or any other factual programme) or listen to a factual radio programme. Then ask them to note down from memory, within a time limit, all the separate items or facts which the programme contained. A comparison of what different children have written should reveal at least one reason why news accounts vary.

Next, ask the children to describe a news item or part of a media presentation from the point of view of a particular person, either someone who is involved in the action or someone who wants to persuade the audience of a particular point of view. A discussion of what they have written should reveal other reasons why news accounts can vary.

The children could ask their parents whether they have any newspaper cuttings of events they themselves witnessed or were involved in. Do they feel the newspaper account was fair and accurate?

Another approach to the question of bias is to take some event that the children have all witnessed or taken part in, maybe some school event or outing or some conflict in the classroom. Activities similar to the above can then be based on this event.

There is also the difficult question of distinguishing between fact and opinion. If you wish to tackle this (perhaps with older children), you could begin with examples. With the help of suggestions from the class, make two lists on the board: the first of statements which are pretty clearly fact (such as 'London is the capital of the United Kingdom'), and the second of statements which are pretty clearly opinion (such as 'Apples are nicer than pears'). Then ask the children to look at newspapers and try to find statements of fact and of opinion. (Reviews of films and plays, for instance, should provide examples in both categories.) This could lead on to a discussion of statements which are a mixture of fact and opinion, or which disguise opinion as fact, though this may well be beyond the grasp of many children.

3.3 FURTHER EXPERIENCE WITH NEWSPAPERS

Looking at advertisements

Bring in a selection of magazines which accompany Sunday papers (or you might ask the children to bring them in). Let the children divide into groups and give each group a magazine. Start by asking each group to pick out four advertisements.

What is each one advertising?
How can you tell that you are looking at an advertisement for a hi-fi system, for instance, rather than a descriptive article about hi-fi systems?
What distinguishes advertisements?

Then encourage the children to look for other advertisements in their magazine and to discuss the ways in which people are portrayed in them, using the questions on p. 63 'Looking at advertisements'. Afterwards the class could come together and talk about their findings. This could lead to a general discussion about how values are expressed by the way we represent things.

Role-playing a situation reported in the news

This activity is recommended only for older children. Choose a news item about a conflict which has not yet been settled. It might be a local debate about the siting of a new road or rubbish tip, for example, or a disagreement between world leaders or different political parties over a particular issue. Ask the children to find out as much as they can about the issue. They are then to prepare a role-play in which they take the parts of the different people/groups involved and explore possible outcomes to the situation. After the role-play the class can make a display explaining the background to the issue and the possible courses of action suggested.

Making scrapbooks

Let the class divide into groups and ask each group to decide upon a theme. Ask the children to collect as many newspaper articles as they can on their chosen theme over a period of time. Themes could include human rights, a particular country, an on-going strike.

Finding out about newspapers

Using children's encyclopedias and books such as some of those listed on p. 53, the children could find out how news is collected, edited and assembled and how papers are printed and distributed. The children could also look up the history of each paper and its present circulation.

A visit to the local newspaper offices would add to the children's interest and understanding, and might give them an opportunity to ask questions about how the paper gathers, selects and edits its news.

Producing a news-sheet

The children must first decide what kind of news and other items they would like to see in their news-sheet. They then need to decide how they want to organize themselves.

Do they want everything decided by everyone?
Or do they want everyone involved in the overall plan and then individuals appointed to undertake specific tasks?
Or do they prefer a hierarchy of control?

If they decide to tackle a local issue they could interview friends and neighbours and compare their views with those expressed in the local paper.

When the news-sheet has been produced, the children might consider questions such as:

Was there any conflict when they were deciding on a structure for organizing the production of the news-sheet? If so, how was it resolved?

Did the structure work? Would they wish to change it if the news-sheet were to be produced regularly?

Was there any conflict between them while producing the news-sheet? If so, how was it resolved?

LOOKING AT ADVERTISEMENTS

Look at the advertisements in your magazine which contain pictures of people and then discuss the following questions:

1 *What kind of people are they?*
   Are they men, women or children?
   How many of them are white?
   How old are they?
   What kind of clothes are they wearing?
   How well off do they look?
   What are they doing?
2 *What products or services are advertised using pictures of men? and of women? and of children?*
3 *Are there any advertisements showing elderly people?*
   If yes, are they men or women?
   What are they advertising?
4 *Why do you think advertisers portray people in the way that they do?*
   What does it tell us about how we see old women, for instance, or short people, or fat people?
5 *Are there any advertisements showing violence? or using violent language? If yes, what are they advertising?*
   If no, why do you think there aren't any in your magazine?
6 *If the world were the way it is shown in advertisements, what would it be like?*

SECTION 4   TELEVISION, CONFLICT AND VIOLENCE

This section stimulates children to think about the television programmes they watch and what they like or dislike in them. It helps them to distinguish between fictional and non-fictional programmes and to think about the conflict and violence in the programmes they watch. They are invited to consider how violence as experienced when watching television may differ from violence as experienced in real life. The children are also encouraged to look at the ways in which television programmes select what to present and how to present it.

This section assumes that the children have worked through at least some of Section 3 and have been introduced to the idea that the media inevitably present a constructed picture of the world. If they have not, you could turn to 'Looking at bias' (p. 60) and undertake some of the activities given there with reference to television. You might also adapt 'Looking at advertisements' (pp. 61 and 63). Further activities on the theme of selecting material for presentation are given on pp. 74–76.

This section can do no more than touch on the large and fascinating field of media studies and media education. It would be well worth exploring this field further with the children, and a few books are suggested under 'Further Resources'.

Children who would prefer to do a project on comics or books, perhaps because they rarely watch television, should be encouraged to do so.

Lesson ideas for the teacher	Activity sheets for the children
4.1 Favourite series and distinguishing between fact and fiction	Favourite series The programmes you watch
4.2 Looking at conflict and violence on television	Violence on television A scene of conflict 1 and 2
4.3 Selecting what to communicate	
4.4 Background notes on children and television violence	

Further Resources

T: for the teacher, C: for the children

BBC, *Violence on television – programme content and viewer perception*, BBC, 1972. (T)

Andrew Bethell, *Viewpoint*, Cambridge University Press, 1979. (T/C)

Lez Cooke (ed), *Media Studies Bibliography*, British Film Institute, 1985. (T)

C Cullingford, *Children and Television*, Gower, 1984. (T)

Derek Heater, *World Studies: Education for International Understanding in Britain*, Harrap, 1980 – Ch 5 'The Teacher and the Media'. (T)

M J A Howe, *Television and Children*, New University Education, 1977. (T)

Colin Jones, *Television*, Franklin Watts, 1980. (C)

Andrew Langley, *Television*, Wayland, 1986. (C)

D Lusted & P Drummond (eds), *TV and Schooling*, British Film Institute, 1985. (T)

Len Masterman, *Teaching about television*, Macmillan, 1980. (T)

G Noble, *Children in front of the small screen*, Constable, 1975. (T)

Colin Reid (ed), *Issues in Peace Education*, D Brown & Sons, 1984 – Richard Keeble, 'Media Images of Violence and Peace'. (T)

M P Winwick & C Winwick, *The television experience: what children see*, Sage Publications, 1979. (T)

4.1 FAVOURITE SERIES AND DISTINGUISHING BETWEEN FACT AND FICTION

It is useful to begin by establishing how much television the children actually watch and what they like. Ask the children to list (without discussion) their five favourite television series and to award each one points out of ten. When they have done this, make a list on the board of all the favourite series, and add up all the points awarded to each series (or ask a small group of children to go round the class and add up the points). Write the results up on the board. The children could then make block graphs to display the information.

This could be followed by a brief discussion:
How did you decide how many points to award each series?
Do you find your favourite series exciting? If so, why?
What goes to make a series good?

The activity sheet 'Favourite series' (p. 68) could be used at this point. (The programme names on it are invented.) Activities similar to the above could be devised for series that the children dislike.

Next, give each child a copy of the activity sheet 'The programmes you watch' (p. 69). Before the children fill in the sheets it is important to make sure they understand the difference between fact and fiction. You could discuss this with them, asking questions such as:

What does 'fiction' mean?
How can you tell whether a book is fact or fiction?
Can you think of any books which are a mixture of fact and fiction?
(*historical novels, for example*)
How can you tell whether a television programme is fact or fiction?
Can you think of any which are not really either fact or fiction, but which are mainly about people's opinions? (*for example, chat shows and discussion programmes*)

If you talk about books or programmes which are a mixture of fact and fiction or which express opinions, the class will need to decide whether to classify these as fact or as fiction when answering the questions on the activity sheet. When the sheets are completed the children can compare and discuss what they have written, perhaps initially in small groups.

In order to compare everyone's responses to questions 1–5, groups of children could collect the responses to these questions and use graphs to display the results. When all the graphs are up on the wall the class can discuss them:

Are there any questions to which most people have given the same answer?
If so, can people explain why they have answered in this way?
Are different people's reasons similar?

FAVOURITE SERIES

GRAPH SHOWING THE THIRD YEAR'S FAVOURITE TELEVISION SERIES

FAVOURITE SERIES	NUMBER OF CHILDREN
	1 2 3 4 5 6 7 8 9 10 11 12 13 14 15
John & Terry	▨▨▨▨▨▨▨▨
Sprinter	▨▨▨▨
Lapwing Lane	▨
Tops of the Pop	▨▨▨▨▨
Mindbender	▨
Around the Clock	▨
Princes of Danger	▨▨▨▨▨▨▨▨▨▨▨▨▨▨▨
The 'G' Gang	▨▨▨▨▨▨▨
Nice Guys	▨
Dragon Lady	▨
Chit-Chat	▨▨▨▨
The Robert Greenway Show	▨▨▨▨▨▨▨▨▨▨
Gremlin for Hire	▨
Rogue Rat	▨▨

1 What is the most popular series?

2 How many children are represented by one square?

3 How many children are there in the third year?

4 Write out the series in order putting the most popular one first.

5 Find the difference in votes between the most popular and the least popular series.

6 Which series has twice as many votes as Dragon Lady?

This page may be photocopied

THE PROGRAMMES YOU WATCH

1 How often do you watch television?
every day ☐   nearly every day ☐
sometimes ☐   never ☐

2 Roughly how much time do you spend watching television after you get home from school?
none ☐   half an hour ☐   one hour ☐
two hours ☐   three hours ☐   four hours ☐
more than four hours ☐

3 Are most of the programmes you watch fact or fiction?
fact ☐   fiction ☐

4 What kind of fiction programme do you like best?
cartoons ☐   comedies ☐   soap operas ☐
science fiction ☐   films and plays ☐

other ☐   say what ....

5 What kind of factual programme do you like best?
news and current affairs ☐   sport ☐   documentaries ☐
science and nature ☐   quiz shows ☐

other ☐   say what ....

6 Do you always know whether what you are watching is fact or fiction?
Yes ☐   No ☐

7 Do you feel different if you know that what you are watching actually happened?
Yes ☐   No ☐

8 What kind of programme do you get most involved in?

....

4.2 LOOKING AT CONFLICT AND VIOLENCE ON TELEVISION

Programmes showing violence

Start with a brief discussion of the kinds of violence shown on television. (If you have not previously discussed what violence is, turn back first to p. 29.) You might raise questions such as:

Which of the following do you count as violent?
wrestling or boxing
a lion killing and eating a zebra
cartoon characters having a fight
two people shouting angrily at each other
What different types of violence can you think of?

Then ask each child to make a list of any programmes or series which in his/her opinion show violence. You may want to limit this to day-time and early evening programmes. It is obviously important not to give children the impression that you want them to go home and watch violent programmes. Rather, you want them to explore the violent aspects of the kinds of programmes most of them regularly watch. If some children say that they do not watch programmes which show violence, suggest that they look for some other characteristic of the programmes they watch (selfishness, for example, or unselfishness).

When the children who are making lists of programmes showing violence have completed them, they could try to answer the questions on p. 71 'Violence on television'. Copies of the page could be given to individuals in preparation for a group or class discussion of the issues raised.

Scenes of conflict

The children should be encouraged to focus on particular scenes of conflict. You might want to limit the choice to children's television to avoid scenes of very violent conflict. Written work and/or discussion could be undertaken:

Written work

The activity sheet 'A scene of conflict 1' (p. 72) suggests various pieces of writing.

Discussion

This could begin by asking the children what scenes of conflict on television stand out in their memory, and seeing if there is any scene that they all remember. If there is, a class discussion can follow. If not, the children could get into groups each of which could discuss a different common scene. Questions for discussion are given on p. 73 'A scene of conflict 2'.

VIOLENCE ON TELEVISION

When you have made a list of scenes which in your opinion show violence, try to answer the following questions:

1 *What sort of programme was each scene in? For instance, was the programme a comedy, a Western, a cartoon, a news bulletin, a documentary or some other kind of programme? How many of these programmes were fiction?*

2 *How do you feel when you are watching a violent scene on television? and after you have watched it?*

3 *Do your feelings depend on what kind of violence it was? or on what kind of programme the scene was in?*

4 *Do any of the programmes showing violence come from one of your favourite series?*
If yes, does the violence appeal to you?
Why, or why not?

5 *Have you ever observed or been involved in any of the sorts of violence you have seen on television?*
If yes, how did you feel?
If you were an observer, was it different from observing similar violence on television?
If yes, in what ways?

A SCENE OF CONFLICT 1

Think of any scene of confrontation that you have seen on television which stands out in your memory.

Keeping that scene in mind, answer the following questions:

1 *Is the confrontation between:*
adults?
children?
adults and children?

Write a short account telling how the confrontation came about.

2 *How is the confrontation settled?*
one person or side exerting force
one person or side giving way
an outside influence
negotiations or discussions

3 *Has the confrontation been settled for good or do you think it could flare up again?*
Give your reasons.

4 *Try to imagine that you are one of the characters in the scene. Write a short piece describing the scene and say what you were feeling at the time.*
or
Imagine that you are a passer-by. Write a short account of what you saw. How did you feel about it?

5 *Was your scene taken from a story, or did it happen in real life?*
If your scene was fiction do you think anything like it could happen in real life?
Explain your reasons for saying YES or NO.

A SCENE OF CONFLICT 2

Make sure that all the people in your group are thinking of the same scene.
Then discuss the following questions:

1 Who is involved in the conflict?

2 What do they each want?

3 Is the scene exciting, or upsetting, or frightening?
If yes, why?

4 Does the scene contain any fighting or killing?
If yes, are the victims shown?

5 Does the scene contain any other forms of violence?

6 If there is violence of any kind, are its consequences shown?
If not, what would they be?
Would the programme have a different impact if the consequences were
actually shown?

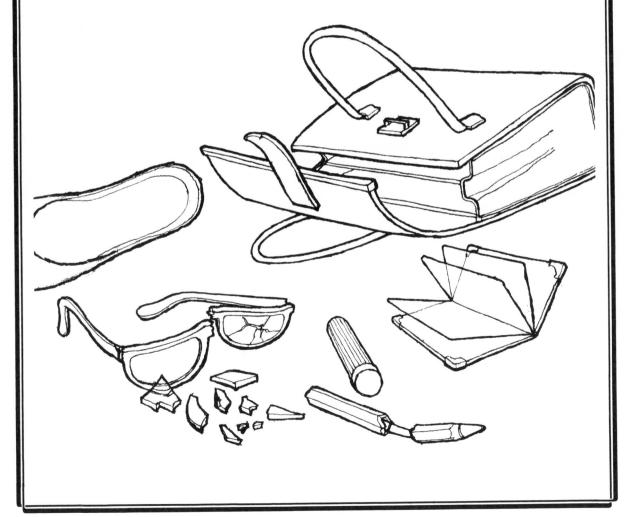

4.3 SELECTING WHAT TO COMMUNICATE

One of the characteristics of conflict and violence on television is that its portrayal is in various ways unrealistic, and the children should be made aware of this. Firstly, of course, there is the general point that presentations of all kinds are selective and may be designed with a certain viewpoint in mind. The camera chooses to focus on one thing rather than another, to film it at a distance or close up, to juxtapose it with something else that gives it a certain significance, and so on. Part of the art of film making, especially in fictional productions, lies in putting information across in subtle ways. For instance, people's dress and manner of speaking tell us important things about them and influence the way we react towards them.

Secondly there is the fact that in many fictional portrayals of conflict and violence their consequences are not shown. The victim is not seen bleeding to death and the violent hero is not shown being sent to prison for criminal actions. Indeed violent behaviour is often exhibited by the hero and associated with success and manliness. Thus there is a danger that children may see the 'exciting' aspects of violence on the screen and fail to realise that, if that violence were happening in real life, the consequences might be far from exciting.

Activities

Below are a few suggestions as to how the children might be introduced to these ideas. Masterman's book contains many more practical activities concerned with teaching about television and, although they are designed for secondary schools, some of them can be adapted for younger children (as has the first activity here).

1 Ask the children to write down all the ways in which they think we can communicate without words. You can then draw up a list on the board from their suggestions. It may help if you bear in mind the following aspects of non-verbal communication: appearance, posture, orientation (direction facing), use of space, facial expression, eye contact, touch, smell and non-verbal aspects of speech (such as noises or dialect). When the list has been drawn up, a discussion should follow:

What can we communicate through our hairstyle, the clothes we wear, how close we come up to people, whether we look them in the eye and so on?

Can you think of examples of ways in which you yourself communicate non-verbally?

Can you think of examples of similar non-verbal messages on television?

2 Ask the children, in pairs, to try and communicate something non-verbally. (See p. 12.)

3 Suggest to the children that they should make a viewing frame with their hands and go round the classroom choosing shots for a film showing:

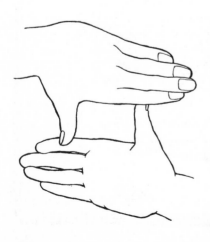

1 What a bright tidy room it is.
2 What a dull untidy room it is.
3 How it is full of busy people.
4 How it is a boring lifeless place.

4 Put up a large painting or poster and encourage the children to suggest questions which one might ask about it. (It does not matter if the questions cannot be given definite answers.) Questions might include:

What is the picture about? Describe it.
What are the objects and events?
When and where is the situation?
Who are the people? How can you tell?
What can you observe about their age, health, clothes, outlook and so on?
What do you imagine the people are feeling?
What might happen next?
What does the picture make you feel?
What kind of mood or atmosphere does it suggest? How does it do so?
How has the artist or photographer composed the picture? What is s/he trying to communicate?
Why do you think the picture is that size and shape? How would it look if it were smaller, for example, or squarer?
How would the picture look if you were viewing it on a colour television? Or on a black and white television?

5 Tell the children that a film is going to be made using the characters from their favourite series and that the film will be shown in the cinema. They are to design a poster giving people who have never seen the series an idea of what the film will be like. Before the children start, discuss briefly the kinds of things they will want to put across.

When they have finished, display the posters and discuss how the children have attempted to put across the essential elements of their series.

How have you selected what to include?
What have you left out?

They could then try and write a short description of their film for insertion in the local newspaper. In both the written description and the poster they will have had to try and select the important points.

What can be put across verbally but not visually? Vice versa? In the actual series, how are things selected? What is left out?

6 See if you can obtain a film poster for a popular children's film. (The Vintage Magazine Shop, 39 Brewer Street, London W1R 3FD sells posters for both current and old films, and runs a mail order service. Or a local cinema may be able to let you have a poster, or tell you where you can buy posters locally.) When the children have all had a chance to look at the poster carefully, you could discuss it with them.

How does it put across the essential elements of the film?
How does it use visual imagery?
Why isn't the poster simply a 'still' from the film?
Is the poster less realistic than a still?

7 Take a popular series which has a hero or heroine. The children are to write a story about the character's activities between the heroic escapades we see on the screen. You will need to discuss this

briefly first in order to emphasize that you do not want more episodes like those on the screen, but rather an account of how the heroes and heroines live their everyday lives. If the heroism includes the use of violence, the account will need to explain how the characters cope with the consequences of their violent behaviour. Do people retaliate? Are the characters sent to prison? Who deals with the damage or suffering they cause? Where does their money come from?

8 Take a popular programme with one or two central characters and ask the children to re-write an episode from the point of view of one of the minor characters, bringing out how this person feels about what is going on. If the minor character is a victim of violence, this could lead to interesting discussion.

9 Use the picture set *Peace, Conflict and Violence* to stimulate further discussion of how artists and photographers communicate with their audiences (see Introduction: footnote).

4.4 BACKGROUND NOTES ON CHILDREN AND TELEVISION VIOLENCE

A large amount of research has been devoted to ascertaining the effects on children of television in general and of violence on television in particular. Different studies have come up with widely differing conclusions and it would be impossible to summarize them adequately here. However a few remarks may be helpful.

It is estimated that over 90% of British children in the 9–12 age group watch television every day, and that the average time spent watching is around 3 hours per day, though more than 20% watch 5 hours or more.

Below are some of the hypothesised effects of television violence on children.

1 It may influence behaviour, especially by encouraging the child to imitate the violence. Imitation is thought to be most likely in cases where the aggressor is rewarded rather than punished for his/her violence, or where the aggression is realistically portrayed.

2 It may influence the child's attitudes to the use of violence. For instance it may encourage the child to believe that acting violently is the normal way of dealing with a range of problems.

3 It may desensitize the child to violence and increase the child's tolerance of violence in others.

4 It may cause the child anxiety, especially in the case of newsreel violence and in cases where the victim's suffering is shown.

5 It may have almost no effect and indeed the child may be unaware that violence has been shown. Verbal acts of aggression and ridicule may create more unease in children than physical aggression, especially if the verbal aggression occurs in circumstances which could apply to their own lives. Seeing a real football match with the home side losing may lead to more anger and frustration then watching a Western.

6 It may have cathartic effects, bringing relief from tension and pent-up emotion. This is most likely where the aggression is stylistic and the victim is not shown (for instance in Westerns).

A few of the many books which deal with the subject of television violence are listed on pp. 65–66.

PART C OTHERS' WORLDS

This part of the book starts by looking at prejudice. It encourages children to realise that although people from other cultures may appear very different in behaviour and lifestyle, they are human beings like ourselves and we all have much in common. Following on from this the children are given the opportunity to study three societies, all rather different from our own, which do not go to war. The aim of such a study is to help the children realise that not all societies make preparation for war or expect to fight wars from time to time. This will encourage them to consider whether or not warfare is natural or inevitable, and thus whether the idea of sustained peace can be more than an unrealisable dream.

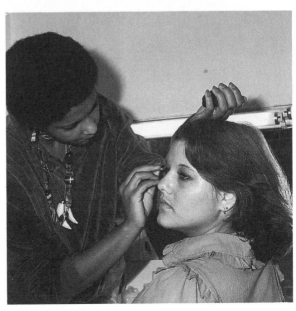

SECTION 5 UNDERSTANDING ANOTHER CULTURE

Prejudice is often based on ignorance of what other people are really like. The aim of this section is to provide a basis for understanding the way of life of other people through an appreciation of some of the similarities and differences between cultures. Direct communication with people in other countries is an obvious way of dispelling prejudice, and practical suggestions for making and sustaining links with foreign schools are included.

Lesson ideas for the teacher	Activity sheets for the children
5.1 The home environment, past and present	Questions to ask older people
5.2 Customs and celebrations at home and abroad	
5.3 Contact with a foreign school	

Further resources

T: for the teacher, C: for the children

Janet Ardavan, *Discovery 7–11 age*, EARO, 1985. (T)

Sylvia Bates, *Religions of the World*, Macdonald, 1979. (C)

Marc and Evelyn Bernheim, *In Africa*, Lutterworth, 1974. (C)

Barbara Clark, *The Changing World and the Primary School*, Centre for World Development Education, 1979. (T)

Cockpit Theatre and Oxfam, *The People G.R.I.D. (Growth, Relationships, Inter-Action, Development) – Three games and activities for ages 8–12 years*, Oxfam, 1980. (C)

W Owen Cole (ed), *World Religions: A Handbook for Teachers*, Commission for Racial Equality, 1982. (T)

Judith Elkin, *Children's Books for a Multi-cultural Society: 8 – 12*, Books for Keeps, 1985. (T)

Kathleen Elliott, *Festivals and Celebrations*, Young Library, 1984. (C)

Simon Fisher, *Ideas into Action – Curriculum for a changing world*, World Studies Project, 1980. (T)

Derek Heater, *World Studies: Education for international understanding in Britain*, Harrap, 1980. (T)

Pictorial Charts Educational Trust, *Annual Festivals – set of posters*. (For address of Trust see p. 160.) (C)

Catherine Storr, *Feasts and Festivals*, Patrick Hardy Books, 1983. (C)

Neil Taylor and Robin Richardson, *Change and Choice: Britain in an Interdependent World*, Centre for World Development Education. (T/C)

Series of books/booklets for children (arranged by publisher):

A & C Black, *Celebrations series* – includes *Dat's New Year, Diwali, Sam's Passover.*

Macdonald, *Religions of the World series* – includes *The Jewish World, The Muslim World, The Sikh World.*

Macdonald Educational, *My First Encyclopedia* (in 10 volumes) –
*Vol 2 Living Together, Vol 3 Different Peoples, Vol 4 Fun and
Games.*

Macmillan, *Patterns of Living* series – includes *City Life, Family Life,
Food for Life, Learning in Life, Village Life.*

Franklin Watts, *I am a ...* series – includes *I am a Greek Orthodox, I
am a Hindu, I am a Muslim, I am a Sikh.*

Wayland, *Festivals* series – includes *Christmas, Easter, Harvest and
Thanksgiving, New Year, Buddhist Festivals, Hindu Festivals, Jewish
Festivals, Muslim Festivals, Sikh Festivals.*

Wayland, *Religions of the World* series – includes *Buddhism,
Christianity, Hinduism, Islam, Judaism, Sikhism.*

5.1 THE HOME ENVIRONMENT, PAST AND PRESENT

Before considering some of the similarities and differences between our lifestyle and that of people in other countries, it is useful to compare our way of life with that of our predecessors. Life in Britain fifty years ago may initially seem less 'strange' to many children than present-day life in a distant country.

A child, comparing two pictures of the same street, one taken recently, the other in 1900, said: 'This looks ordinary, that one doesn't.' 'Ordinary' can mean different things to different people. Children can be encouraged to appreciate this by looking closely at their own surroundings, noting those things which they take for granted, and making a comparison with what their grandparents were familiar with. They could devise questionnaires about their grandparents' childhood, incorporating questions such as those on p. 84 'Questions to ask older people'.

A visit to the school by a grandparent might stimulate discussion. If there is a local museum with costumes or other objects from the period, a class visit would be valuable. It is important to bring out the fact that the way of life fifty years ago seemed entirely normal at that time.

Complementing the questionnaire, an exhibition could be arranged with photographs showing what life was like about fifty years ago. It could include pictures of important events such as holidays and weddings. Children might be able to bring along exhibits loaned by older members of their families. Or a local museum might sell reproductions of old photographs or postcards.

The exhibition could be brought to life if each photograph or object from the past were displayed beside a complementary example from the present.

QUESTIONS TO ASK OLDER PEOPLE

Here are some questions you might ask your grandparents or other older people to help you find out what life was like when they were at school. You can add more questions of your own.

1 *What did you do at school?*
2 *What was your classroom like?*
3 *Did you have lunch at school?*
4 *What did you eat for lunch?*
5 *What did you do when you got home from school?*
6 *What was your favourite form of entertainment?*
7 *What music did you like? And where did you hear it?*
8 *Did you get pocket money? If so, what did you spend it on?*
9 *How was your home heated?*
10 *Where did you go on holiday? How did you get there?*
11 *How did you celebrate Christmas? Birthdays?*
12 *What were your favourite presents?*

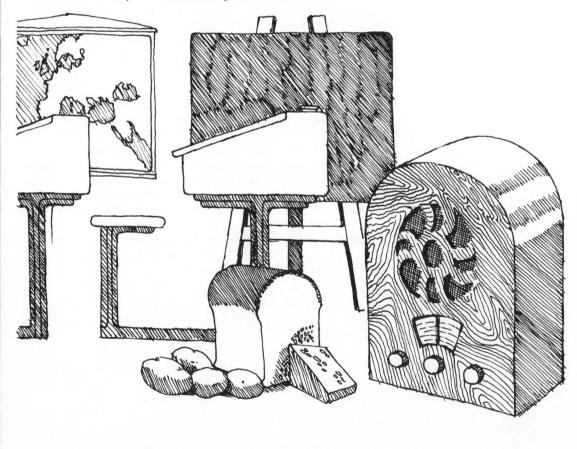

5.2 CUSTOMS AND CELEBRATIONS AT HOME AND ABROAD

The customs and celebrations of any country are often a strong visual example of its culture, and before expanding the topic to look at other societies, the children could benefit from exploring our own customs (perhaps as part of R.E. lessons). Important events in our own year – birthdays, Christmas, weddings – could be discussed or written about (or even celebrated), and if there are differences already existing within the class between children of varying cultural backgrounds, these could provide valuable material.

With this preparation, the class could now start to consider the customs and celebrations of other countries. It should be emphasised that their customs are as ordinary for the people taking part in them as our customs are for us. From the point of view of classwork, this exploration could be divided into religion and customs.

Religion

There is much in common between Christianity, Judaism and Islam. Parts of the story of Joseph could be read from Ch.12 of the Koran as well as from Genesis Ch. 37–45 to show that the three faiths have some common heritage. (The Old Testament is of course common to Judaism and Christianity.) A class visit could be made to the nearest Synagogue or Mosque, during which aspects of the religion such as basic beliefs, celebrations, clothes, food and the form of the religious services could be explained and discussed. Alternatively, this could be done by a visitor coming to the class.

Other major religions such as Hinduism, Buddhism and Sikhism could be studied, especially if there are people from those religious groups in the class or the locality. There is a wealth of recently published books for children on the major religions and their festivals. (See pp. 81–82.)

Customs

The customs and celebrations of other countries have obvious potential as an art topic. The children could pick one particular celebration, such as Karneval in the Rhineland, a West Indian carnival, the Jewish Passover, Chinese New Year, Diwali (Hindu Festival of Light, also a Sikh festival). They could make a colourful display showing how the festival is celebrated. If the festival lends itself to costume and mask making, the children might like to dress up, and they might even organise their own school carnival along similar lines, if appropriate.

Another approach is to compare similar celebrations in different countries, such as weddings or New Year. It might also be possible to invite visitors from local religious or cultural groups or from abroad to talk about these special events.

These studies might well conclude with a discussion, during which some of the following points might be considered.
What do the customs and celebrations of the different countries have in common?
Do the celebrations fulfil similar functions?
Are the differences partly due to geographical factors like climate and lifestyle?
How might the different customs have originated?

5.3 CONTACT WITH A FOREIGN SCHOOL

Misconceptions about fundamental aspects of other cultures can lead to prejudice. Direct contact with a school in a different part of the world can help to dispel such prejudice. By comparing and contrasting what their counterparts see as 'ordinary', the children in both countries can help undermine the attitude that what is unknown is threatening. The similarities between the children's own lives and those of their counterparts can help them to understand that we are all members of the human race and as such have much in common.

The timetable for such a project might be as follows:

1 Make contact with a foreign school. (See p. 88.) It is important to be clear at the outset what kind of exchange you are hoping for.

2 When contact has been made with the other school, ask the children to introduce themselves and their lives by means of drawing, painting, writing or photographs. Suggest that the children from the other school introduce themselves in a similar way. Mailings should be arranged so that the parcels cross in the post.

3 While waiting for the parcel to arrive, ask the class to prepare descriptions and pictures of what they imagine the lives of the other children to be like.

4 When the parcel arrives, the material can be displayed alongside the children's imagined impressions, and the class should be encouraged to discuss or write about any discrepancies between the two.

5 Slides or films of the other country might be obtained, or a speaker familiar with that country be invited to the school, in order to enlarge the children's picture of it.

Contact with the other school could be developed in various ways. The children could send things which give some idea of their everyday life, such as postcards, newspaper cuttings, a copy of the school magazine, books, artwork, maps, diaries, weather information, stamps, typical recipes, dried flowers and leaves and maybe examples of local crafts.

Each child could be paired with one (or more) of the foreign children and correspondence encouraged. For instance, the children could communicate about their families, their friends and their interests and hobbies. They could send photos of themselves and maybe tape-recordings of their voices or of their favourite music. If the foreign children understand English, the children in your class could get into pairs and each child could write a description of his/her partner as well as of him/herself. Thus the children would be able to send descriptions of themselves as others see them as well as their own descriptions of themselves. If language is a barrier, the children will have to communicate in other ways, which should help them learn a lot about non-verbal communication. If the foreign language uses a different alphabet, the children might like to learn its letters.

In order to maintain a link it is important that the intervals between your communications with the other school should not be too great. Surface mail can be very slow, so it is a good idea to use air mail where possible. A steady flow of material is much more valuable than an occasional large parcel. The higher the quality of the material you send, the better the chances of a successful and worthwhile link.

How to make initial contact with a foriegn school

If you do not happen to have personal contacts through whom you can get in touch with a school in some other country, you will obviously need to go through an agency or organisation. It may be useful to choose a country about which the children already know a little (or at least think they do!), because they may then already have prejudices about it. If you live in a town which is twinned with one or more foreign towns, there may be a Twinning Committee which can help you. An account of one person's experience with an African school is included on p. 90.

Some organisations which may be able to help you make contact with a foreign school are listed below. Details of other organisations can be found in the booklet *Overseas Development and Aid: A guide to sources of information and material*. This is available free of charge from the Overseas Development Adminstration, Eland House, Stag Place, London SW1E 5DH.

The Central Bureau for Educational Visits and Exchanges
Seymour Mews House, Seymour Mews, London W1H 9PE
The Bureau arranges links with schools in many parts of the world, though the majority of their links are with European and American schools. The application form is accompanied by suggestions for

activities such as exchanges of scrapbooks and tape-recordings, and notes on how a link can be valuable in different subject areas.

The Commonwealth Linking Trust
Seymour Mews House, 2nd Floor, 26–37 Seymour Mews, London W1H 9PE
The Trust establishes links between schools throughout the Commonwealth. The application form is accompanied by a very useful leaflet on how to make your link a success. It includes practical matters, such as checking that any parcel you send will not attract customs duty, as well as many suggestions for things to exchange.

The British-Soviet Friendship Society
36 St Johns Square, London EC1V 4JH
The Society runs a pen-friend service for its members and has local groups which may be able to help you. If you do not want to join the Society, you could try writing direct to the USSR. Every Soviet city has a 'Society for cultural and friendly exchanges with foreign countries'. Simply put on the envelope the above plus the name of your chosen city. (If Russian is taught in any of the local schools, they might be able to translate your letter, but that is not essential.) It is best to start by suggesting something simple and unproblematic, such as an exchange of artwork between schools. The Society may take quite a while to reply, though you are likely to get a quicker response if you write to one of the smaller cities, rather than, say, Moscow or Leningrad which already have plenty of foreign enquiries.

The Fulbright Commission
6 Porter Street, London W1M 2HR
The Commission can provide addresses of U.S. state boards of education, which you can write to for possible contacts in their states. It also has a directory of both private and state schools in the U.S. which you can look at in its office.

Impressions of Africa: One person's account of a school link

A class of ten year-olds were invited to write down everything they associated with the word 'Africa'. The result was predictable: lots of animals, in deserts and jungles. No-one mentioned villages, towns or cities; there were no roads, railways or airports.

We then produced essays and drawings by pupils from a secondary school in Zambia, sent by ex-students from Keswick Hall College of Education, who were teaching there. The effect was remarkable:

Can Africans write in English?
They write better than us!
Don't they draw nicely?
Aren't the people working hard?
This essay says, 'My village is fantastic!'
They catch lots of fish – but none of us wrote down 'fishing'.
There's a school in this village.
My picture shows a bus stop, too!

Africa had been transformed from a remote and hostile place to a place with real people in it. The class drew pictures and wrote about their commuter village; the package was posted to Zambia and we are hoping that the exchange will continue and develop further. It was certainly one of the most successful and enjoyable practical lessons on Education for International Understanding that I can recall. Some pen-friendships are now developing (greatly helped by the colourful stamps on the envelopes!). But even without the pen-friend element, the idea of understanding other people through their own writing and drawing seems a helpful one.

Below are a few extracts from the children's letters telling about the various villages they come from.

'My village is situated on the bank of the river Zambezi. It is known as Lusile which means civilised people. Mostly the people in my village are farmers who keep cattle herds.'

'Mine is a big village with twenty-two houses, ten made out of bricks and the rest made out of mud and grass on top. The people in my village are co-operative and happy too. They love each other and do helpful things in the village. More than twelve people are farmers and five are fishermen. Majority of boys in my village are educated. We have six boys at the University of Zambia and five are working on high posts in the republic of Zambia.'

'We got a wonderful ceremony which took place every year in March when the plain is over flooded. This ceremony is called Kuomboha, which means the removal of the Lozi people from the lowland to highland. Of course we have three bars, one with a cocktail, and a rest house and two restaurants. During night time you can go for entertainments like films, disco, dance that is every night.'

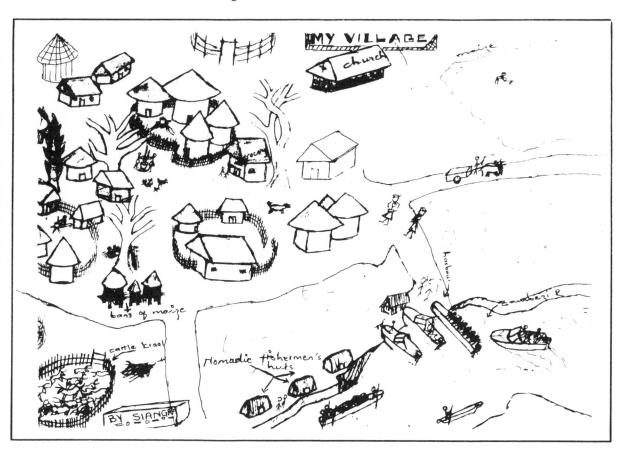

SECTION 6 PEACE AND CONFLICT IN OTHER SOCIETIES

Most people would prefer peace to war. The major world leaders frequently talk of their desire for peace. Yet there always seems to be a war being fought somewhere in the world. Is that because warfare is natural to the human race, or somehow an inevitable product of society? Could warfare in fact be avoided altogether? In other words, is sustained peace an impossible dream or could it become a reality?

This section does not attempt to explore the whole of this complex issue. It simply aims to provide evidence that societies which do not go to war do exist. Such evidence obviously tends to make us question the idea that warfare is inevitable.

Three societies have been chosen for study: the South Fore of New Guinea, the Trobriand Islanders and the Costa Ricans, but others could be added. For instance, the Inuit (Eskimos) are another example of a people which does not go to war. It might also be valuable to study a very warlike society, such as the ancient Assyrians. (See p. 97 for relevant literature.)

The fact that the three societies described here have not indulged in warfare for considerable periods of time does not of course prove that peace could be achieved world-wide. One could argue that because the societies are small or dispersed or in developing parts of the world their achievements in respect of peace are not relevant to large industrialized nations. Nevertheless the fact that these societies have enjoyed sustained periods without war, or preparation for war, does provide some hope that the quest for peace is not futile. In particular it challenges the idea that warfare is an inevitable product of human nature. This idea is obviously linked to theories about aggression being innate and violence natural.

The children will not be in a position to enter fully into this debate. However, when aspects of the subject come up in discussion it is worth bearing in mind the different senses in which the word 'aggression' can be used. In its narrow sense it means ' unprovoked or unjustified attack'. In its wider sense it means 'self-assertiveness' or 'attack' generally, without implying any moral judgement. When people say that aggression is innate, they usually mean either that a tendency to attack others is inborn, or simply that self-assertiveness is a natural characteristic that can be used for good or ill. It can be argued that aggression in the sense of self-assertiveness is natural and healthy, but that problems arise when the aggressiveness expresses itself in acts of violence. The question is then: Is it part of human nature to sometimes express aggressiveness in acts of violence or is violence a learned response, and hence avoidable? Even if one believes that violent behaviour is inevitable, it does not necessarily follow that warfare is inevitable. It has been argued that warfare is a human invention not a biological necessity. Some useful books on this subject are given on p. 95.

It is best if each of the societies to be studied can be introduced via something concrete which is within the child's own experience. One approach is to start by talking about some article which we import from the other country, or from that part of the world. For instance, we import coffee from Costa Rica, and you may be able to buy sweet potatoes (though not necesarily from New Guinea). Bananas and coconuts are of course readily available, and you could talk about the kinds of places from which they come and why they are only grown in certain parts of the world. This could lead, through the consideration of climate, to the subject of New Guinea (including the Trobriand Islands) and Costa Rica, all of which grow bananas.

If you know anyone who has been to any of the countries, they might be able to lend some object(s) which they have brought back, or stamps which may show something of the life of the country. Even better, the person might be willing to bring the items in themselves and talk to the children. Stamp collectors in the class may also be able to bring in stamps, or you could probably buy a few quite cheaply. Stamps often present a colourful image of their country, and merit examination under a magnifying glass. Older children could look out for references to a particular country in the newspapers.

How you use the information on each society which is given here will depend largely on the age and ability of the children. Older children may be able to read it for themselves. With a younger class you may want to read it to them, or else put the essential information across in other ways.

You might like to divide the class into three groups, each studying a different society (or more than three groups if extra societies are included). If you do this, it will be particularly important for the children to produce informative displays, so that everyone can benefit from the research carried out by each of the groups. The groups could also devise verbal or dramatic presentations.

Lesson ideas for the teacher	Information and activity sheets for the children
6.1 The South Fore	The South Fore of New Guinea Learning to be non-aggressive Anger and aggression Map of New Guinea area
6.2 The Trobriand Islanders	The Trobriand Islanders and their cricket A Peace Conference in Sarawak A Trobriand cricket match Feelings in connection with sport
6.3 Costa Rica	Costa Rica: a country without an army Finding out about Costa Rica Costa Rica as seen by its politicians Central America: soldiers and teachers National expenditures

6.4 Concluding discussion

Further resources
T: for the teacher, C: for the children
General
Carmarthen Development Education Centre, *A Rainforest Child: An activity based teaching pack*, Green Light Publications. (T/C)

John Ferguson, *War and Peace in the World's Religions*, Sheldon Press, 1977. (T)

Simon Fisher and David Hicks, *World Studies 8–13: A Teacher's Handbook*, Oliver and Boyd, 1985. (T)

Derek Heater, *World Studies: Education for International Understanding in Britain*, Harrap, 1980. (T)

D Hicks and C Townley (eds), *Teaching World Studies: An Introduction to Global Perspectives in the Curriculum*, Longman, 1982. (T)

Edward H Jones *et al.* (ed), *Aggression*, Routledge & Kegan Paul, 1972. (T/C)

Ashley Montagu (ed), *Man and Aggression*, Oxford University Press, 1968. (T)

Gerald Priestland, *The Future of Violence*, Hamish Hamilton, 1974. (T)

Colin Reid (ed), *Issues in Peace Education*, D Brown & Sons, 1984 — especially Mary Midgley, '*The Debate over Aggression*'. (T)

Neil Taylor and Robin Richardson, *Change and Choice: Britain in an Interdependent World*, Centre for World Development Education. (T/C)

Norman Tutt (ed), *Violence*, HMSO, 1976. (T)

Colin Ward, *Violence: its nature, causes and remedies*, Penguin Education ('Connexions' Series), 1970. (T/C)

Sara Woodhouse, *Your Life My Life – An Introduction to Human Rights and Responsibilities*, Writers and Scholars Educational Trust, 1980. (T/C)

David and Jill Wright, 'Teaching about distant environments', in David Mills (ed), *Geographical Work in Primary and Middle Schools*, The Geographical Association, 1981. (T)

South Fore

Dougal Dixon, *Forests*, Franklin Watts, 1984. (C)

Dougal Dixon, *Jungles*, Hamish Hamilton, 1984. (C)

Europa Publications, *The Far East and Australasia* (annual periodical). (T)

Terry Jennings, *The Young Geographer Investigates Tropical Forests*, Oxford University Press, 1986. (C)

Ashley Montagu (ed), *Learning Non-Aggression*, Oxford University Press, 1978 – especially E R Sorenson's paper, 'Co-operation and Freedom among the Fore'. (T)

Gillian Morgan, *Jungles and People*, Wayland, 1982. (C)

Sue Wagstaff, *Kolo's Family*, A & C Black, 1978. (C)

The Trobriand Islanders

For additional books for the children, see those on forests and jungles in the previous section.

Philip Goodhart and Christopher Chataway, *War without Weapons*, W H Allen, 1968.

J Hargreaves (ed), *Sport, Culture and Ideology*, Routledge & Kegan Paul, 1982. (T)

V and P Hereniko, *The Pacific Islanders*, Wayland, 1985. (C)

Jerry Leach and Gary Kildea, *Trobriand Cricket: An ingenious response to colonialism*, 1976 – colour film, 52 mins, available from Concord Films Council Ltd. (T/C)

Bronislaw Malinowski, *Argonauts of the Western Pacific*, Routledge & Kegan Paul, 1922. (T)*

Bronislaw Malinowski, *Coral Gardens and their Magic*, George Allen and Unwin, 1935. (T)*

Richard D Mandell, *The First Modern Olympics*, University of California Press, 1976. (T)

Annette B Weiner, *Women of value, men of renown: New perspectives in Trobriand Exchange*, University of Texas Press, 1976. (T)

*These books contain many interesting black and white photographs which might be useful for the children.

Costa Rica

Barclays Bank, *Costa Rica Country Report* – in regularly updated file of Country Reports. (T)

Richard Biesanz, *The Costa Ricans*, Prentice Hall, 1982. (T)

Leonard Bird, *Costa Rica – A Country without an Army*, Northern Friends Peace Board. (T)

Europa Publications, *South America, Central America and the Caribbean*, 1986. (T)

Keith Lye, *Let's go to Central America*, Franklin Watts, 1985. (C)

World of Information, *Latin America and Caribbean Review* (annual publication). (T)

Different perceptions of army life (see p. 116 for suggested poems and prose passages)
  1 Leonard Clark (ed), *Sound of Battle*, Pergamon, 1969.
  2 Anthony Collins (ed), *War*, Pergamon, 1968.
  3 John Ferguson (ed), *War and the Creative Arts*, Macmillan, 1972 (Open University Set Book).
  4 A E Housman, *Collected Poems*, Jonathan Cape, 1939.
  5 Ministry of Defence, leaflets available from local Army Careers Information Offices (see 'Army' in the phone book), eg *Army Air Corps, Army of the 80's, Get into this world – Women's Royal Army Corps, Guards, The Punch!, Royal Signals*.
  6 Martin Page (ed), *For Gawdsake Don't Take Me! The Songs, Ballads, Verses, Monologues etc of the Call-Up Years 1939-1963*, Hart-Davis, MacGibbon, 1976.*
  7 Martin Page (ed), *The Songs and Ballads of World War II*, Panther, 1975. *
  8 Roy Palmer (ed), *The Rambling Soldier – Military life through soldiers' songs and writings*, Penguin, 1977.
  9 I M Parsons, *Men Who March Away*, Chatto & Windus, 1978.
  10 Herbert Read (ed), *The knapsack, A Pocket book of Prose and Verse*, Routledge and Sons, 1939.
  11 Victor Selwyn (ed), *Poems of the Second World War*, Dent, 1985.

*The language used in some of the writings makes them unsuitable for use in schools.

Other Cultures

British Museum Publications, *The Wars of Ashurbanipal*. (C)

R J Cootes and L E Snelgrove, *The Ancient World*, Longman, 1970. (C)

Education Development Centre (Cambridge, Massachusetts), *Man: A Course of Study*. (Includes a section on the Inuit.) Available via the Centre for Applied Research in Education, University of East Anglia, Norwich NR4 7TJ. (T/C)

Derek Fordham, *Eskimos*, Macdonald Educational, 1979. (C)

David Frankel, *Ashurbanipal and the head of Teumann*, British Museum Publications, 1977. (C)

J H Greg Smith, *Eskimos : The Inuit of the Arctic*, Wayland, 1984. (C)

Marvin Harris, *Cows, Pigs, Wars and Witches – The Riddles of Culture*, Fontana, 1977. (T)

Ashley Montagu (ed), *Learning Non-Aggression*, Oxford University Press, 1978 – especially Jean L Briggs' paper, '*The Origins of Non-violence – Inuit Management of Aggression*'. (T)

R J Unstead and W Forman, *The Assyrians*, Ward Lock, 1980. (C)

6.1 THE SOUTH FORE

Background

The South Fore (pronounced Foray) described here live in a small part of the Eastern Highlands of New Guinea. Although some of the Fore and other Highland peoples are renowned for their warlike character, the groups studied by E R Sorenson were very peaceable. The account given here is based on Sorenson's article 'Co-operation and Freedom among the Fore' (in Montagu's book *Learning Non-Aggression*). The book contains fascinating studies of seven tribal societies. Montagu concludes from these studies that whatever genetic potentialities we may have for aggressive behaviour, early conditioning in co-operative behaviour and the discouragement of anything resembling aggressive behaviour serve to make an individual, and a society, essentially non-aggressive and co-operative.

Before they start on the activities suggested here, the children should be familiar with the contents of the information sheets (pp. 100-101).

Activities

1 Make copies of the activity sheet 'Learning to be non-aggressive' (p. 102). Children could either write their own answers to the questions, or they could discuss them in small groups.

2 Encourage the children to discuss their own experience of anger and aggression. Discussion could be stimulated by first giving them copies of the activity sheet 'Anger and aggression' (p. 103). They could answer the questions individually and then discuss their responses with a partner before coming together for a class discussion.

3 Ask the children to find out more about Papua New Guinea (perhaps from an encyclopedia or a geography book). There are a large number of different peoples in Papua New Guinea and it is unlikely that the children will actually find references to the Fore. However they should be able to find out about the climate, vegetation, crops and wild life of Papua New Guinea. In particular they could try to discover what kind of birds, marsupials and rodents are found there, and what the sweet potato is. (They may be able to read about how sweet potatoes are grown in elliptical mounds, centuries old, and how this cultivation technology is beginning to become popular in the UK under the name of 'deep bed' gardening.) The children could also find out about tropical forests in general. When they have finished their research they can make a pictorial display about Papua New Guinea, including a map showing relief and, if possible, pictures of the countryside and vegetation. The display could include a list of ways in which the life of the Fore (both adults and children) differs from our own.

4 If you feel very confident about your relationship with the children, you could attempt to give them an unannounced experience of overcrowding so that they can see how they respond. Move them all to one side of the classroom and ask them to get on with some work there. There will be inevitable discomfort and arguments about ownership of space. Appeals will probably be made to you (as authority figure) to settle disputes. Afterwards the children could discuss how they felt when they were cramped and how they treated each other as a result. You could also ask the

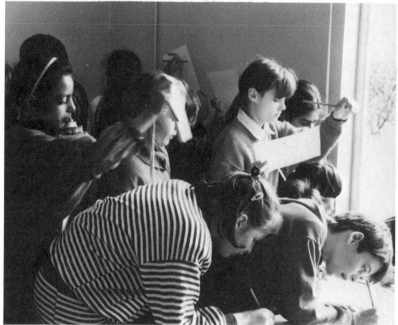

children how far they feel their lives are dependent on co-operation and how far on obedience to authority.

NB As you are probably aware, some of the older books which children may find in libraries may be rather patronising about people whom the authors regard as 'primitive' and in need of 'civilization'. This is especially true of books about people like the New Guinea Highlanders, many of whom, unlike the Fore, are/were quite aggressive and warlike. Such an approach obviously tends to discourage children from seeing the people as intelligent human beings with cultures and values of their own.

THE SOUTH FORE OF NEW GUINEA

The South Fore (pronounced Foray) live in parts of the Eastern Highlands of Papua New Guinea (see map p. 104). This is an area of tropical forest. They live in hamlets and hunt for birds, marsupials and rodents. They also grow sweet potatoes and other vegetables. However their gardens and hamlets are not permanent. When the piece of land which they have been cultivating loses its fertility, they clear a new piece of forest and start again.

The South Fore do not have chiefs, priests, medicine men or other authority figures. From early childhood onwards each person enjoys a great deal of personal freedom, but the people also co-operate closely with one another. The South Fore are remarkable in that there is very little conflict and aggression among them. Even children rarely quarrel or fight, and babies seldom cry. The people tend to be co-operative and affectionate and they spontaneously share food and work.

How does this peaceable way of life come about? The answer seems to lie, at least in part, in the way in which the children are brought up. Babies are in physical contact with other people almost all the time. They spend most of their days in their mother's lap or being carried by her or other people, and they are not put down when mother is busy. Thus all their basic needs, such as food, security and stimulation, are continuously satisfied. This close physical contact seems to encourage an intuitive understanding between the child and those who care for it, and this kind of understanding of each other is evident among Fore people of all ages. As the baby grows older it is allowed to explore its surroundings freely. Fore children are not told what to do and what not to do. They learn this by observing and being in touch with people around them. Because there are no commands to obey, children cannot disobey and be 'naughty', so this source of conflict does not exist. Children feel free and unfrustrated, so they do not have to rebel. They also feel secure and loved.

Nevertheless young Fore children are sometimes aggressive either by accident or simply to 'see what happens'. In such cases the child is not punished. The usual reaction is amusement. If the child's aggressive actions become painful or damaging, the person attacked normally either moves away or else tries to distract the child and interest it in something else. In this way anger, squabbling and fighting do not become a natural part of life. Conflict between adults is usually dealt with by one person or party simply moving away from the scene of conflict. This could mean anything from going for a walk to moving to distant lands.

The peaceable way of life described here seems to survive among the Fore so long as there is plenty of virgin land to which to move if problems arise. In areas where new land is no longer abundant and different groups have to compete for it, conflict increases and fighting may break out.

We know about the way of life of the South Fore because an anthropologist, Richard Sorenson, went to live among them for a while and filmed many of their activities. One of his conclusions is that aggression is determined by culture. People are not 'naturally' aggressive or non-aggressive. Whether they grow up to act aggressively or non-aggressively depends on their culture, upbringing and circumstances.

LEARNING TO BE NON-AGGRESSIVE

In several societies in other parts of the world, children are brought up to be non-aggressive. Here are some examples of how the Fore prevent aggressiveness from developing.

If playing gets rough, or children get angry, either some of them will move away or adults will distract those who are being aggressive. Affection rather than scolding is used.

Fore children usually react to attack by younger children with affection and amusement. If the attack gets painful, they either move away or try to interest the younger child in some other activity.

The drawings show how two Fore children deal with aggressiveness from a toddler.

Toddler picks up stick.

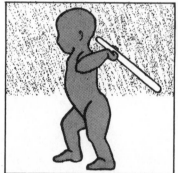
Toddler hits girl.

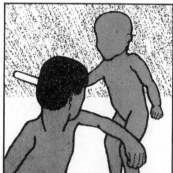
Girl laughs.

Girl catches stick and throws it away.

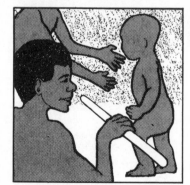
Boy distracts toddler.

Toddler moves to boy to be picked up.

How would you behave if you were in the girl's position?

Do you ever deal with a conflict simply by moving away from it? If so, in what kind of situation? If not, is there a reason why you don't?

ANGER AND AGGRESSION

Think about occasions when you have felt angry or aggressive. Then try to answer the questions given here:

1 *What makes you feel angry?*
2 *When you feel frustated about something, do you find yourself getting angry?*
3 *What do you do when you feel angry?*
4 *Do you ever attack other people, either physically or verbally? If yes, in what kind of circumstances?*
5 *Could those circumstances be avoided or prevented?*
6 *Do you think you could go through life without ever expressing anger or attacking people?*
7 *Could you go through life without even feeling angry?*
8 *Why do you think the Fore seem to be able to live so non-aggressively?*

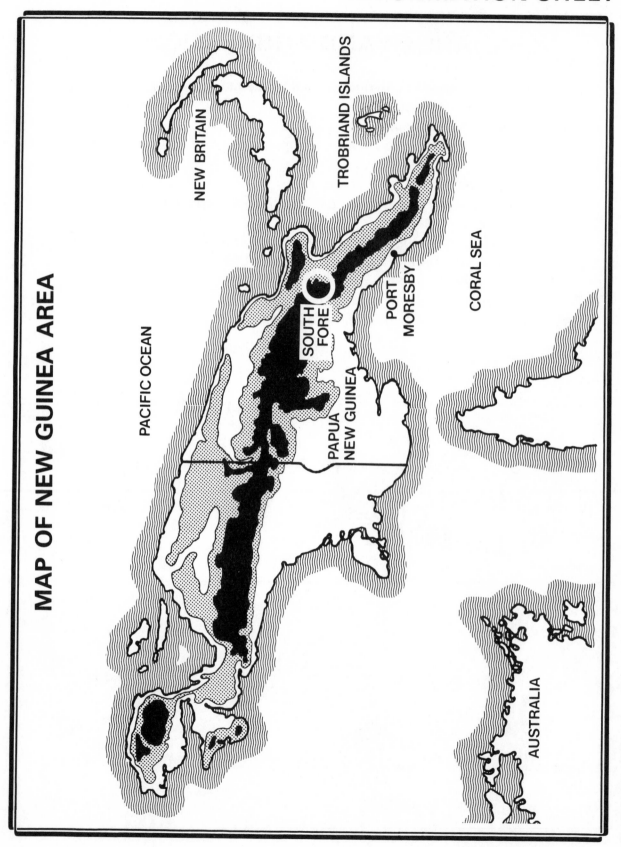

MAP OF NEW GUINEA AREA

NEW BRITAIN

TROBRIAND ISLANDS

PACIFIC OCEAN

SOUTH FORE

PORT MORESBY

PAPUA NEW GUINEA

CORAL SEA

AUSTRALIA

This page may be photocopied

6.2 THE TROBRIAND ISLANDERS

Background

There is a wealth of information on the Trobriand Islands in the writings of Bronislaw Malinowski and others. The information provided here on Trobriand cricket was obtained from the film 'Trobriand Cricket: An Ingenious Response to Colonialism' (see p. 96). The passage quoted is taken from the first part of the film. The film is not suitable to be shown in full to the children. It would be best if you viewed it first, and then showed them the second half (beginning with the preparations for the cricket match). The children should be familiar with the contents of the information sheets (pp. 108–9) before they see the film, otherwise they may find it hard to understand. You should also give them a list of things to look out for such as those suggested on the activity sheet 'A Trobriand cricket match' (p. 113).

One subject which you may like to discuss with the children is the idea of sport being a force for peace. In the Trobriand Islands and in Sarawak sport has enabled former enemies to compete in a friendly way. The founder of the modern Olympic Games, Baron de Coubertin, saw them as a great step forward in the cause of peace and hoped that 'the spirit of international comity may be advanced by the celebration of their chivalrous and peaceful contests.' However, the Games have now become a forum for patriotic fervour and it has been argued that, far from fostering international harmony, the modern Olympics encourage nationalism and international rivalry.

George Orwell once described international sport as 'war minus the shooting'. If we agree with this description, does it mean that international sport develops aggressive and warlike behavior? Or could it mean instead that sport allows already existing aggression to be expressed in a relatively harmless manner? People who believe the latter tend to think that aggression (in the sense of a tendency to attack others) is innate and has to find expression in some form. Whereas people who believe the former feel that international sport creates or develops feelings of rivalry and aggression which otherwise would not exist.

It is important to distinguish sport as experienced by the spectator from sport as experienced by the participant. In international sport the spectators feel that they are being represented by their country's athletes and sportsmen and women. Their national pride is at stake, and they tend to see the competitors from other countries chiefly as rivals to their own. The competitors themselves, on the other hand, have at least the opportunity of seeing their rivals also as individual human beings with whom they could become friendly. In a similar way, a football match between two schools may provide an opportunity for children from those schools to get to know each other a little.

Other questions which might come up in discussion include the problem of violence among football spectators and the role of competition in sport. If you want to develop the topic of sport, peace and violence you could look at the books suggested on pp. 95–96. However it is important not to get so involved in this aspect of sport that others such as physical exercise, playfulness and co-operation are forgotten.

Activities

1 Before the children see the film, give them the questions on p. 113 'A Trobriand Cricket Match' so that they can look out for the information they require. When they come to answer the questions, they may want to work in groups as they are unlikely all to have remembered everything they need. The children's drawings and paintings can later become part of a display about the Trobriand Islanders and their cricket.

2 Ask the children to find out more about the Trobriand Islands. As they are small islands which form part of the state of Papua New Guinea, the children are unlikely to find descriptions of the Trobriand Islands in particular. However, they can find out about climate, vegetation, crops and wildlife in Papua New Guinea in general and they can draw a map of the Trobriand Islands. They may also find relevant information by looking up 'Pacific Islands' or 'South Sea Islands'. The results of their research can be presented as a display along with the follow-up work to the film.

3 The whole class could try playing a game of Trobriand cricket. This could include face painting and other forms of decoration. If the school has woodwork facilities it might be possible to make and decorate a Trobriand-style cricket bat. If not, an ordinary cricket or rounders bat could be used, perhaps decorated with black and white tape. The children must remember to bowl with a bent arm as if throwing a spear. They could devise their own chants and dances around whatever is topical, as the Islanders sometimes do.

4 Trobriand cricket is not the only example of tribes competing in sport instead of war. On p. 110 is the story of how a Cambridge man

working in Borneo introduced a boat race to the local inhabitants. As the account is rather long and wordy, it is probably best if you re-tell it to the children in your own words.

5 Discuss some of the roles which sport can play. The discussion could be based on the activity sheet 'Feelings in connection with sport' (p. 114), which you could give to the children beforehand.

THE TROBRIAND ISLANDERS AND THEIR CRICKET

The Trobriand or Kiriwina Islands lie off the south-east coast of mainland Papua New Guinea (see map p. 104). The islanders live in villages set in clearings in the low dense jungle, and one of their main activities is growing food. Their crops include yams, taro, bananas, coconuts and sugar cane. The big villages have a large circular space in the middle which is used for public ceremonies and festivities such as dancing and feasts. This space is surrounded by two concentric rings of houses: the inner one consists of houses in which yams are stored, while the outer one is made up of dwelling huts. These are dark and stuffy inside as there are no windows, but they are used only at night or in wet weather. Cooking and eating normally take place in the circular street between the houses.

In 1903 the Rev Mr Gilmour, a Methodist missionary, arrived in the Trobriand Islands. This was at the time when the Australians were establishing control over the area, and Mr Gilmour was one of the first white people to arrive in the Trobriand Islands. Traditionally the different groups on the islands had indulged in warfare against one another from time to time, but the government wanted to put a stop to this. Mr Gilmour helped to abolish fighting by teaching the islanders to play cricket. He introduced the game partly as entertainment and partly as a substitute for warfare and to encourage a new morality.

At first the islanders played cricket the way they were taught, but one of them has described how this soon changed. 'Polite non-political competition didn't last long. Villagers played a few games against the converts and then they made it our kind of competition. They got rid of the twelve player business and the whole community played as one team. If forty players came, forty played on each side, if fifty came, fifty played – with ritual display and gifts of food underlying it all. . . . Gilmour's wickets were higher with spaces between the stumps and there were short sticks on top of the wickets – bails. But later on people got rid of them and used hand bails. People closed and shortened the stumps. And used magic. Batsmen used to run. But now they each have a runner. Runners dash to get their sticks over the crease line. [The runners carry thin sticks.] They made smaller bats and balls, and put a curve in the bat for better hitting.'

The cricketers began to dress as if for war and various rituals were introduced which were formerly used in warfare. The use of magic became important both before and during the game. Cricket in the Trobriand Islands now looks very different from the game that was introduced in 1903. The bats, which are carved out of light hard wood, are decorated in the traditional war colours: black and white. Before the game the teams treat their bats with magic, in much the same way as warriors used to use magic to fortify their spears. Magic is also used for protecting wickets, for distracting opponents, for preparing the arms and hands of the bowlers for accurate throwing and for changing the course of the ball. Before the match the players decorate themselves by painting their faces and bodies, much as they used to do before going into battle. They may also adorn themselves with necklaces, anklebands, feathers and other decorations.

Dancing accompanied by chanting used to be important in warfare and it has now become an essential part of playing cricket. From the moment the players parade on to the field, chanting and dancing, to the moment the game is over and they make their exit in the same manner, the game is periodically stopped for ritual performances. These may contain both traditional and modern elements. For instance, if a man is caught out, the triumphant team may sing 'P.K.' This chant and dance originated from the Wrigleys P.K. Chewing Gum introduced by the Australians and relates the surehandedness of the fielders to the stickiness of chewing gum. The words of the chant are 'So strong was it shot [by the bat] but P.K. are my hands! I am P.K.! I am P.K.!'

Trobriand Cricket has an economic and political significance. It is played in the harvest season, and the host village needs to grow extra food so that there is enough for the feasting which follows the matches. Calling a cricket season is one way of earning a political reputation. A number of visiting teams come and play against the host, and the matches are followed by a ceremony in which the teams exchange gifts of food.

A PEACE CONFERENCE IN SARAWAK

The extract below is taken from *The Eagle*, a magazine of St John's College, Cambridge. It was written about 1900. The story takes place in the basin of the river Baram on the island of Borneo, in Sarawak (Malaysia). The Resident is a Mr Charles Hose, an old Cambridge man and friend of the author of the article. Mr Hose is ruling over the Baram district.

The peace-making that I am going to describe was organised by [the Resident] in order to bring together on neutral ground and in presence of an overwhelming force of the tribes loyal to the government all those tribes whose allegience was still doubtful, and all those that were still actively hostile to one another, and to induce them to swear to support the Government in keeping the peace and to go through the formalities necessary to put an end to old blood feuds. At the same time the Resident had suggested to the tribes that they should all compete in a grand race of war-canoes, as well as in other races on land and water. For he wisely held that in order to suppress fighting and head-hunting, hitherto the natural avenues to fame for restless tribes and ambitious young men, it is necessary to replace them with some other form of violent competition that may in some degree serve as a vent for high spirits and superfluous energy, and he hoped to establish an annual gathering for boat racing and other sports, in which all the tribes should take part, a gathering on the lines of the Olympic Games in fact. The idea was taken up eagerly by the people, and months before the appointed day they were felling the giants of the forest and carving out from them the great war-canoes that were to be put to this novel use, and reports were passing from village to village of the many fathoms length of this or that canoe and the fineness of the timber and workmanship of another.

In order to make clear the course of events, I must explain that two large rivers, the Baram and the Tinjar, meet about one hundred and thirty miles from the sea to form the main Baram river. Between the banks of these two rivers and their tributaries there is a traditional hostility which just at this time had been raised to a high pitch by the occurrence of a blood-feud between the Kenyahs, a leading tribe of the Baram, and the Lirongs, an equally powerful tribe of the Tinjar. In addition to these two groups we expected a large party of the Madangs, a famous tribe of fighting men of the central highlands whose hand had hitherto been against every other tribe, and a large number of Dayaks, who, more than all the rest, are always spoiling for a fight, and who are so passionately devoted to head-hunting that often they do not scruple to pursue it in an unsporstsmanlike fashion. So it will be understood that the bringing together in one place of large parties of fully armed warriors of all these different groups was a distinctly interesting and speculative experiment in peace-making.

The place of meeting was Merudi, the headquarters of the government of the district. There the river, still nearly a hundred miles from the sea, winds round the foot of a low flat-topped hill, on which stand the small wooden fort and court house and the Resident's bungalow. Some days before that fixed for the great meeting by the tokens we had sent out, parties of men began to arrive, floating down in the long war-canoes roofed with palm leaves for the journey. On the appointed day some five thousand of the Baram people and the Madangs were encamped very comfortably in leaf and mat shelters on the open ground between our bungalow and the fort, while the Dayaks had taken up their quarters in the long row of Chinamen's shops that form the Merudi bazaar, the commercial centre of the district. But as yet no Tinjar folk had put in an appearance, and men began to wonder what had kept them – Were the tokens sent them at fault? Had they received friendly warnings of danger from some of the many sacred birds, without whose favourable omens no journey can be undertaken? Had they, perhaps, taken the opportunity to ascend the Baram and sack and burn the houses now well nigh empty of defenders? We spent the time in foot-racing, preliminary boat-racing, and in seeing the wonders of the white man. For many of these people had not travelled so far down river before, and their delight in the piano was only equalled by their admiration for that most wonderful of all things, the big boat that goes upstream without paddles, the Resident's fast steam launch.

At last one evening, while we were all looking on at a most exciting practice-race between three of the canoes, the Lirongs, with the main mass of the Tinjar people, came down the broad, straight reach. It was that most beautiful half-hour of the tropical day, between the setting of the sun and the fall of darkness – the great forest stood black and formless, while the sky and the smooth river were luminous with delicate green and golden light. The Lirongs were in full war dress, with feathered coats of leopard skin and plumed caps plaited of tough rattan, and very effective they were as they came swiftly on over the shining water, sixty to seventy warriors in each canoe raising their tremendous battle-cry, a deep-chested chorus of rising and falling cadences. The mass of men on the bank and on the hill took up the cry, answering shout for shout, and the forest across the river echoed it until the whole place was filled with a hoarse roar. The Kenyahs ran hastily to their huts for their weapons, and by the time they had grouped themselves on the crest of the hill, armed with sword and shield and spear and deadly blowpipe, the Lirongs had landed on the bank below and were rushing up the hill to the attack. A few seconds more and they met with a clash of sword and shield and a great shouting, and in the semi-darkness a noisy battle raged. After some minutes the Lirongs drew off and rushed back to their boats as wildly as they had come, and strange to say no blood was flowing, no heads were rolling on the ground, no ghastly wounds were gaping, in fact no-one seemed any the worse. For it seems that this attack was merely a well-understood formality, a put-up job, so to say. When two tribes, between whom there is a blood feud not formally settled, meet together to make peace, it is the custom for the injured party, that is the tribe which has last suffered a loss of heads, to make an attack on the other party but using only the butt ends of their spears and the blunt edges of their swords. This achieves two useful ends - it lets off superabundant high spirits, which if too much bottled up would be dangerous, and it 'saves the face' of the injured party by showing how properly wrathful and bellicose its feelings are. So when this formality had been duly observed everybody seemed to feel that matters were going on well and they settled down quietly enough for the night, the Resident taking the precaution to send the Lirongs to camp below the fort, and the great peace conference was announced to be held the following morning.

Soon after daybreak the people began to assemble beneath the great roof of palm-leaf mats that we had built for a conference hall. The Baram chiefs sat on a low platform along one side of the hall, and in their midst was Tama Bulan, the most famous of them all, a really great man who has made his name and influence felt throughout a very large part of Borneo. When all except the Tinjar men were assembled, of course without arms, the latter, also unarmed, came up the hill in a compact mass, to take their places in the hall. As they entered the sight of their old enemies, the chiefs of the Baram, all sitting quietly together, was too much for their self-control; with one accord they made a mad rush at them and attempted to drag them from the platform. Fortunately we white men had placed ourselves with a few of the more reliable Dayak fortmen between the two parties, and partly by force and partly by eloquence we succeeded in beating off the attack, which seemed to be made in the spirit of a school rag rather than with bloody intent. But just as peace seemed restored a great shout went up from the Baram men, 'Tama Bulan is wounded', and sure enough there he stood with blood flowing freely over his face. The sight of blood seemed to send them all mad together; the Tinjar people turned as one man and tore furiously down the hill to seize their weapons, while the Baram men ran to their huts and in a few seconds were prancing madly to and fro on the crest of the hill, thirsting for the onset of the bloody battle that now seemed the matter of a few seconds only. At the same time the Dayaks were swarming out of the bazaar seeking something to kill, like the typical Englishman, though not knowing which side to take. The Resident hastened after the Tinjars, threw himself before them, and cursed and appealed and threatened, pointing to the two guns at the fort now trained upon them, and Tama Bulan showed his true greatness by haranguing his people, saying his wound was purely accidental and unintended, that it was a mere scratch, and commanding them to stand their ground. Several of the older and steadier chiefs followed his example and ran to and fro holding back their men, exhorting them to be quiet.

The crisis passed, the sudden gust of passion slowly died away, and peace was patched up with the interchange of messages and presents between the two camps. The great boat race was announced to take place on the morrow, and the rest of the day was spent in making ready the war canoes, stripping them of their leaf roofs and all other superfluous gear.

At daybreak the racing boats set off for the starting post four miles up river. The Resident had given strict orders that no spears or other weapons were to be carried in the racing boats, and as they started up river we inspected the boats in turn, and in one or two cases relieved them of a full complement of spears, and then we followed them to the post in the steam launch. There was a score of entries, and since each boat carried from sixty to seventy men sitting two abreast, more than a thousand men were taking part in the race. The getting the boats into line across the broad river was a noisy and exciting piece of work. We carried on the launch a large party of elderly chiefs, most of whom were obviously suffering from the 'needle', and during the working of the boats into line they hurled commands at them in language that was terrific in both quality and volume. At last something like a line was assumed, and on the sound of the gun the twenty boats leaped through the water, almost lost to sight in a cloud of spray as every one of those twelve hundred men struck the water for all he was worth. There was no saving of themselves; the rate of striking was about ninety to the minute, and tended constantly to increase. Very soon two boats drew out in front, and the rest of them, drawing together as they neared the first bend, followed hotly after like a pack of hounds. This order was kept all over the course. During the first burst our fast launch could not keep up with the boats, but we drew up in time to see the finish. It was a grand neck-and-neck race all through between the two leading boats, and all of them rowed it out to the end. The winners were a crew of the peaceful down-river folk, who have learnt the art of boatmaking from the Malays of the coast, and they owed their victory to the superior skill in fashioning their boat rather than to superior strength. When they passed the post we had an anxious moment – how would the losers take their beating? Would the winners play the fool, openly exulting and swaggering? If so they would probably get their heads broken, or perhaps lose them. But they behaved with modesty and discretion, and we diverted attention from them by swinging the steamer round and driving her through the main mass of the boats. Allowing as accurately as possible for the rate of the current as compared with the rate of the tide at Putney, we reckoned the pace of the winning boat to be a little better than that of the 'Varsity eights in facing over the full course.

The excitement of the crowds on the banks was great, but it was entirely good-humoured – they seemed to have forgotten their feuds in the interest of the racing. So the Resident seized the opportunity to summon everyone to the conference hall once more. This time we settled down comfortably enough and with great decorum, the chiefs all in one group at one side of a central space, and the common people in serried ranks all round about it. In the centre was a huge, gaily painted effigy of a hornbill, one of the birds sacred to all of the tribes, and on it were hung thousands of cigarettes of home-grown tobacco wrapped in dried banana leaf. Three enormous pigs were now brought in and laid, bound as to their feet, before the chiefs, one for each of the main divisions of the people, the Barams, the Tinjars and the hill-country folk. The greatest chiefs of each of these parties then approached the pigs, and each in turn, standing beside the pig assigned to his party, addressed the attentive multitude with great flow of words and much violent and expressive action, for many of these people are great orators. The purport of their speeches was their desire for peace, their devotion to the Resident ('If harm come to him, then may I fall too', said Tama Bulan), and their appreciation of the trade and general intercourse and safety of life and property brought them by the Rajah's government, and they hurled threats and exhortations against unlicensed warfare and bloodshed.

A TROBRIAND CRICKET MATCH

Read these questions before you see the film so that you can look out for the information you need. Afterwards you can answer them through writing, drawing and painting.

1 *What do the men wear when they are playing cricket?*
2 *What do the women wear?*
3 *What are the houses like?*
4 *What kind of trees grow in the Trobriand Islands?*
5 *Name one thing that the people eat. Can you find out more about it?*
6 *How many players were there in the game which was filmed?*
7 *What do the bats look like?*
8 *How many paces are there between the wickets?*
9 *What did the visiting team base their entrance dance on?*
10 *What parts of Trobriand Cricket are based on war rituals?*
11 *Make a list of all the differences you noticed between British and Trobriand cricket.*

FEELINGS IN CONNECTION WITH SPORT

1 *Do you enjoy playing sport? Why, or why not?*

2 *Do you enjoy watching sport? Why, or why not?*

3 *What is your favourite/least favourite sport? Why?*

4 *Do you ever express angry feelings when playing sport? If yes, do you actually hurt anyone (physically or verbally)? Or are your angry feelings directed at something like the ball?*

5 *How do you feel about the other side while playing a team game?*

6 *Can your feelings change after the game is over?*

7 *Are your feelings about the other side different if you are a spectator?*

8 *Do you ever play non-competitive sport? If yes, do you enjoy it?*

9 *Do you think sport can encourage friendship and co-operation in our part of the world?*

This page may be photocopied

6.3 COSTA RICA

Background

Since the political situation in Central America is not very stable, you may need to check that the information given here is still correct. The Central America Information Service publishes a bi-monthly fact sheet giving up-to-date information on Costa Rica, and Barclays Bank produces regular 'Country Reports'. The quotations on p. 120 are taken from Leonard Bird's booklet on Costa Rica.

Before they start on the activities suggested here, the children should be familiar with the contents of the information sheets (pp. 117–118).

Activities

1 Encourage the children to find out more about Costa Rica. Children's encyclopedias are often a good source of information. Suggested questions are given on the activity sheet 'Finding out about Costa Rica' (p. 119).

2 Give the children the information and activity sheets 'Costa Rica as seen by politicians', 'Central America: soldiers and teachers' and 'National expenditures' (pp. 120–122).* A discussion should follow, based on questions such as:
What does this information tell us about Costa Rica's priorities?
Do you agree with Charpentier that a defenceless country is less likely to be attacked than an armed one?
What is a developing country?
Which of the countries on p. 122 are developing countries?

You should explain that developed countries generally have higher public expenditures per capita than developing countries, and so Israel's 4% spent on health actually represents more money per capita than Costa Rica's 22%.

3 Let the children divide into small groups, preferably with even numbers in each group. Half the group is to imagine they are Costa Ricans, and the other half are Britons. Set the scene for an informal meeting – perhaps a British family is on holiday in Costa Rica and has been invited to lunch by a Costa Rican family. They are each talking about their country and after a while they come to the topic of defence. The Costa Ricans explain the advantages of not having an army while the Britons talk of the advantages of having one.

When the groups have completed their role plays, they might like to swop around so that those who were playing Costa Ricans now play Britons, but with a new 'family' as their opposite number.

The class can then come together for a discussion.
Did you find it easier to play one nationality rather than the other?
Were you swayed by the other side's arguments?
What is your own opinion?

4 There is a wealth of poetry and prose describing the glory, horror, boredom and many other aspects of war. A comparison of different perceptions of life in the army could provide a link between this section of the book and the Armistice Day Assembly (p. 155). A selection of poetry and prose which might be suitable is given here. The numbers in brackets refer to books listed on p. 96 in which the

* The figures on pp. 121 and 122 are for 1983

writings may be found. These books obviously contain further relevant material. Leonard Clark's selection of poems about war for 9-15 year olds, *Sound of Battle*, contains so many suitable poems that they cannot be listed here. If you can find a copy of this book, you will be able to make your own selection. Additional suggestions for poems and songs may be found on p. 158.

Anon., *From A Dying Soldier To His Love*. (7)
Anon., *If*. (6)
Anon., *I wanna go home*. (6)
Anon., *Light Horse*. (8)
Anon., *Mother's song*. (7)
Anon., *The Soldier's Return from India*. (8)
Anon., *Why?* (6)
Peter Appleton, *The Responsibility*. (2, 3)
John J Blockley, *The Scarlet and the Blue*. (8)
Sergeant Bourgogne, *Hunger*. (10)
David Stafford Clark, *Casualty*. (11)
William Cobbett, *The Pangs of Hunger*. (8)
Grady and Hazel Cole, *The tramp on the street*. (3)
Joy Corfield, *First Night in Barracks*. (11)
W Gibson, *Breakfast*. (2)
Tony Goldsmith, *The G I at War*. (11)
Julian Grenfell, *Into Battle*. (10)
Thich Nhat Hanh, *Condemnation*. (3)
A E Housman, *Epitaph on an Army of Mercenaries*. (3, 4)
Kenneth Mould, *Night Clothing*. (11)
Siegfried Sassoon, *Suicide in the Trenches*. (2, 9)
Pete Seeger, *Where have all the flowers gone?* (3)
Sergeant Taffs, *One of the Horrors of War*. (8)
Unknown Aviator, *War Birds (No.163)*. (10)
W B Yeats, *An Irish Airman foresees his death*. (2, 3)

COSTA RICA:
A COUNTRY WITHOUT AN ARMY

Costa Rica is a small country in Central America. Among the most important crops are coffee, sugar, cocoa and bananas, and large quantities are exported. Industries include metal processing, furniture, building materials, and paper and printing. There are areas of rain forest rich in plant and animal life, but these are increasingly being destroyed to create pasture for beef cattle. Unfortunately the soil is usually poor and so cattle can be grazed on it for only a limited number of years before it is exhausted.

Central America is generally an area of political instability and so it may seem remarkable that Costa Rica has survived without an army since 1948. The decision to disband the army came after the ending of six weeks of fierce civil war in which many people were killed. The fact that people were appalled by the death toll was an important factor leading to the declaration that a standing army was henceforth to be illegal. However this does not mean that Costa Rica is a pacifist nation. It has an extensive police force, part of which is armed. The 1949 amended constitution says that military forces may be organized, but only through continental agreement or for national defence, and in either case they shall always be subordinate to civil power.

There have been a number of situations since 1948 which might have provoked Costa Rica to restore its army, but in fact it has tended to try and resolve the situations through diplomatic means. For instance, two attempted invasions were dealt with by appealing to the Organisation of American States which succeeded in ending hostilities and thus avoiding war.

Costa Rica has developed an important role in promoting world peace through international forums and devotes a large share of its national resources to development. It took a lead in promoting peace at the United Nations Special Session on Disarmament in 1978. The head of the Costa Rican delegation spoke of his country as one which 'is truly disarmed, which works in peace, and at the end of the day can rest with an easy conscience.'

His speech also showed Costa Rica's pride in its democratic tradition and in the fact that having no army enables it to spend more on education, health and social development. He said 'I represent a very special nation and people which . . . have achieved a high level of stability, peace, freedom and justice. . . . I represent a very special nation and people which have achieved a balanced and steady rate of economic and social development.'

Later in 1978 the President of Costa Rica proposed to the United Nations that a University for Peace should be created in Costa Rica. This was chartered by the United Nations General Assembly in 1980. The Costa Rican government donated 700 acres of land, of which 500 is to be preserved as virgin forest and provides a resource for courses in ecology and environmental education. The university is now running courses on matters relating to peace, and students from all over the world are encouraged to attend. The aims of the university include:

promoting among all human beings the spirit of understanding, tolerance and peaceful co-existence

stimulating co-operation among peoples

helping to lessen obstacles and threats to world peace and progress.

The symbol on the university's literature shows a dove encompassing the globe. Beneath this is written 'If you desire peace, prepare for peace.'

Costa Rica has shown considerable commitment to avoiding war and promoting peace and disarmament. However it faces increasing pressures from outside to strengthen its military capabilities, and since 1981 the United States has been providing training for the Civil Guard (the section of the police force which maintains law and order).

No-one can know what the future will bring, but it seems that there would be little popular support for restoring an army. A British visitor reports a recent conversation with a Costa Rican friend in which he asked 'Does any political party advocate having an army?' to which his friend replied, 'No. No-one would vote for them if they did.'

FINDING OUT ABOUT COSTA RICA

1 *What sort of climate does Costa Rica have?*

2 *What is the landscape like? How does it vary from one area to another?*

3 *How many different crops can you find out about? Describe them.*

4 *What do the people eat?*

5 *How many different industries can you find out about? Describe them.*

6 *What language do the people speak?*

7 *Why is the country called 'Costa Rica'?*

8 *What form of government does Costa Rica have?*

9 *What is the national sport?*

COSTA RICA AS SEEN BY ITS POLITICIANS

'SIX GYMNASIUMS cost a million dollars, which is equivalent to the cost of the cheapest warplane of the type being purchased by countries like ours in the Third World. It is more consistent with the Costa Rican tradition to build six gymnasiums than to buy a warplane for Costa Rica.'

The President of Costa Rica, 1977

'When you think about it, we're just a little defenceless country, and it would probably be a simple matter to invade us. But this, believe it or not, is where I believe our strength lies. Could you imagine what the international reaction would be if a purposely defenceless nation were attacked by a heavily-armed one? It would be a shame that would be hard to live down. I think this is the key. Our vulnerability makes us strong.'

Minister Charpentier, 1976

'Costa Rica is one of the poorest countries in Central America in natural resources, yet it has a
* higher income, literacy rate, and life expectancy
* better health facilities
* and lower infant mortality rate
than most countries in Latin America.
Due to our disarmament, we have been able to develop the country faster.'

Ambassador at the UN Special Session on Disarmament, 1978

CENTRAL AMERICA: SOLDIERS & TEACHERS

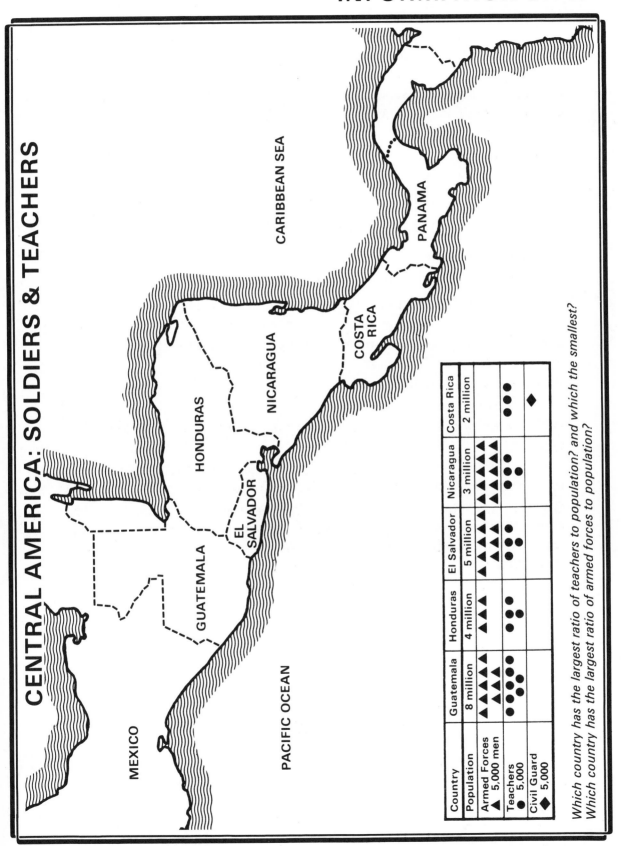

MEXICO

PACIFIC OCEAN

GUATEMALA

HONDURAS

EL SALVADOR

NICARAGUA

COSTA RICA

PANAMA

CARIBBEAN SEA

Country	Guatemala	Honduras	El Salvador	Nicaragua	Costa Rica
Population	8 million	4 million	5 million	3 million	2 million
Armed Forces ▲ 5,000 men	▲▲▲▲▲▲▲	▲▲▲	▲▲▲▲▲▲▲▲	▲▲▲▲▲▲▲	
Teachers ● 5,000	●●●●●●●	●●●	●●●●●	●●●●	●●●
Civil Guard ◆ 5,000					◆

Which country has the largest ratio of teachers to population? and which the smallest?
Which country has the largest ratio of armed forces to population?

NATIONAL EXPENDITURES

The figures below show what percentage of government spending goes on education, health and defence.

	Education	Health	Defence
Costa Rica	19	22	3*
Great Britain	12	11	11
Israel	7	4	26
Papua New Guinea	21	9	4

* Rural and Civil Guards

Display this information on a graph, and then answer the following questions:

1 Which country gives the largest percentage of government spending to
   a) education   b) health   c) defence

2 Which country gives the smallest percentage of government spending to
   a) education   b) health   c) defence

3 Which country spends almost equal amounts on education, health and defence?

4 Both Israel and Jordan give about a quarter of their government spending to defence. Why do you think they both spend so much on defence?

5 Great Britain actually spends more money per person on education and health than the other three countries. Does this tell you anything about the total amount of money spent per person?
   If so, what?

6.4   CONCLUDING DISCUSSION

When the children have completed their study of the three societies, you should bring them together for a discussion. Obviously the form this takes will depend partly on their age and level of understanding and partly on whether the whole class studied each of the societies or whether they divided into groups. If each child has studied only one of the societies, the children may first want to question each other about the displays. Subsequent discussion could focus on questions such as:

Do the three societies have anything in common?
How do they differ from each other and from our society?
What do we have in common with them?
Can we learn anything from them?
Could we adopt similar attitudes to aggression and war? If so, how? If not, why not?

PART D OUR WORLD

This part looks again at the themes of conflict and change and relates them to the future of our world. The children explore different ways in which change can come about, and are encouraged to think not only of their own personal futures but also of the future of the planet as a whole. They are introduced to the idea of peaceful or non-violent action as a tool for change through studying people such as Mahatma Gandhi and Cesar Chavez. It is hoped that, by the time they have worked through the book, children will have a greater understanding of the consequences of violence and the possibilities of non-violence; also that they will feel confident in their potential to bring about change and influence their own future.

SECTION 7   CHANGE AND THE FUTURE

This section considers some of the changes that might come about in the children's lifetimes and some of the consequences of different possible futures. The children start by exploring the concept of change. They are then encouraged to use their imagination to create a variety of pictures of the future. The aim is to help children appreciate that we are living in a rapidly changing world, to widen their vision of the possibilities open to the human race and to encourage them to feel that they can have some influence over what happens in their lifetime.

Lesson ideas for the teacher	Activity sheets for the children
7.1 Change	
7.2 The Futures Game	
7.3 Images of the future	Life in twenty years' time The Future 1 & 2

Further Resources

T: for the teacher, C: for the children

Bernard Benson, *The Peace Book*, Jonathan Cape, 1981. (C)

Peter Campbell, *The Environment*, Oliver & Boyd, 1985. (C)

Children of Hiroshima Publishing Committee, *Children of Hiroshima*, 1981. (C)

Diagram Group, *Earthship*, Longman, 1980. (C)

Nigel Dudley, *Energy*, Ladybird, 1981. (C)

Simon Fisher and David Hicks, *World Studies 8–13: A Teacher's Handbook*, Oliver & Boyd, 1984. (T)*

J Gribbin, *Future Worlds*, Abacus, 1979. (T)

David Lambert, *Planet Earth 2000*, Purnell, 1985. (C)

David Lambert, *Pollution and Conservation*, Wayland, 1985. (C)

Mark Lambert, *The Future for the Environment, Future Sources of Energy, Living in the Future, Transport in the Future*, Wayland, 1985 & 1986. (C)

John Leigh-Pemberton, *Disappearing Mammals*, Ladybird, 1973. (C)

Mike Lyth, *The War on Pollution*, Priory Press, 1977. (C)

Robin Richardson, *Caring for the Planet, World in Conflict*, Thomas Nelson, 1977. (T/C)

James Stachan, *Energy Today: Future Sources*, Franklin Watts, 1985. (C)

Sara Woodhouse, *Your Life My Life – An Introduction to Human Rights and Responsibilities*, Writers and Scholars Educational Trust, 1980. (T/C)

World Studies Project, *Learning for Change in World Society – Reflections, Activities, Resources*, World Studies Project, 1976. (T)

Youth Environmental Action, *Up Your Street*, available from 173 Archway Road, London N6. (T)

* A few of the activities in this section are adapted from the Interim Paper *World Studies 8–13: Some Classroom Activities* which preceded the above book.

7.1 CHANGE

Different kinds of change

Introduce the children to the theme of change by having a
'brainstorm' on changes that have occurred in the past week: at
school, at home or in the neighbourhood. Do this by writing
'Changes in the Past Week' at the top of the board or on a large
sheet of paper. Ask the children to offer any idea that comes into
their heads in connection with this theme. Write up each idea as
briefly as possible. All ideas should be accepted, however ridiculous,
and no-one may comment on any idea at this stage. This process
often brings out imaginative ideas. When a good number of changes
have been written up, call a halt and ask for suggestions as to how
the changes might be grouped. You might need to prompt the
children with questions such as:

Who or what brought about these changes?
Were they planned? Or did they happen by accident, or through
natural causes?
Have any of the changes brought about improvements? If so, for
whom?
Did the changes meet with opposition?

This should lead to a discussion of different kinds of changes, such
as:

natural/unnatural
predictable/unpredictable
planned/unplanned
popular/unpopular
for the better/for the worse (from whose point of view?)

The children could then go home and ask their parents what has
changed in their way of life since they were children. Do they prefer
their present way of life? From their parents' replies the class could
draw up a list of changes that have taken place in the past twenty-
five years or so. They could divide them into some of the different
kinds of change they discussed earlier, which will involve
considering questions such as 'Which changes do they regard as
improvements?'

Time-lines

Let the children divide into small groups and give each group a large
piece of paper with a line ruled across it. This line represents the
past fifty years. Ask the children to mark along the line in words or
pictures the main changes which have occurred in this time. They
can draw on the research they did in Section 5.1 on life in their

grandparents' childhood as well as the research they have just done on life when their parents were children. When they have finished, the groups can compare their time-lines and discuss them. Has the pace of change increased?

The activity can be extended with a time-line from the present to twenty-five or fifty years in the future. The children should mark on the changes that they believe might happen in this time. They could then compare these with the changes in the past fifty years.

7.2 THE FUTURES GAME*

The Futures Game aims to make children aware of the vast range of possible kinds of society and to help them realise that some choices may preclude other choices (for instance a society may not be able to enjoy both a high energy consumption and freedom from pollution). The game starts by letting the future be determined by chance, and then moves on to exploring the role of rational choice in the shaping of the future.

Setting the game up

Start by discussing ways in which societies can differ, and draw up a list of the principal aspects of a society. These could include:

Food production
Housing
Defence
Health Care
Political System
Education
Transport
Communication
Energy production

Choose five of these which seem important and relevant to the children. (A shorter and simpler version of this game could be devised using fewer aspects and/or fewer systems for each aspect.) In the sample game which follows, the first five aspects have been chosen.

Within each aspect, ask the children to suggest different possible systems and choose six for each aspect. Alternatively you can use the sample list given here, though the systems will require discussion to ensure that the children understand them. It does not matter if some of the systems are quite unrealistic. The idea is to stretch the children's imagination.

A sample list of systems:

FOOD PRODUCTION
1 Small traditional farms
2 Large mechanized farms
3 Food from the sea
4 Hunting and gathering
5 Convenience food
6 Synthetic food pills

HOUSING
1 Megacities
2 Towns
3 Villages
4 Isolated huts
5 Tents/teepees
6 Underground dwellings

DEFENCE
1 No defence
2 Militia only
3 Private armies
4 Standing army, defensive only
5 Standing army, offensive and defensive
6 Individual combat by representatives**

HEALTH CARE
1 None
2 Private hospitals and doctors
3 State Health Service
4 Witch doctors
5 Barefoot doctors

6 Computer-run 'expert systems'

** as in the story of David and Goliath

*This game is partly based on 'Futures', a card game devised by Gill Collins, Craig Fletcher and Clive Jones of the School of Architecture, Hull College of Higher Education, 1978/9.

POLITICAL SYSTEM
1 Rule by King or Queen (absolute monarchy)
2 Rule by parliament (parliamentary democracy)
3 No government (anarchy)
4 Rule by world parliament (global democracy)
5 Rule by mothers (matriarchy)
6 Rule by children (puerocracy)

Selecting random futures

When lists such as the above have been agreed upon and written up so that the whole class can see them, the game can begin. It is best played in small groups.

The players select one system from within each aspect. This can be done by throwing a die or by writing all the different systems on slips of paper and drawing one from each set out of a hat.

When one system has been selected for each aspect, the class or group discusses how a society with these systems might work. Fanciful solutions may be accepted so long as people are prepared to defend them. For example, the society might have synthetic food pills, tents, private armies, witch doctors and a king or queen. How could such a society function? The immediate answer might be that it could not function at all, in which case the children could discuss why. Which system(s) do not fit?

The group is allowed up to three more dice throws or draws from the hat in order to try and get a more compatible set of systems. For instance, if the food system is the odd one, the selection for 'FOOD PRODUCTION' may be repeated. If the new system fits better than the original one, a new selection may be made for one of the other aspects (if desired). If not, the selection for 'FOOD PRODUCTION' may be repeated again.

Once the final selection has been made, the children must try to invent an imaginary situation in which these systems could co-exist. For instance, if people live in tents they are unlikely to have the technology to produce synthetic food pills. But maybe they import them because they are convenient for nomadic life. In that case, they must export something. Maybe the witch doctors gather rare plants which the more technological society needs for making drugs. Such ideas could be extended to explain the place of the other systems.

Making choices about the future

When each group has discussed its randomly selected future, ask the children whether they could improve on it by making deliberate choices concerning their future society. What choices would they make? They should consider each aspect in turn and vote for the system they prefer within it. The number of votes should be recorded against each of the systems. The group's chosen future will be made up of the five most popular systems. They should discuss this future and those who did not vote for a particular system can ask its supporters to defend it.

Concluding discussion

At the end, the class should come together again for discussion:
What kinds of things happen because people choose them?
What kinds of things happen randomly?
What kinds of things happen because other people impose them?
Can we produce a better future through choice than by random means?
Would it be possible to eliminate all random happenings?

7.3 IMAGES OF THE FUTURE

Life in twenty years' time

Having explored imaginative futures, the children could now focus on more realistic and specific possibilities. In order to stimulate them to imagine what life might be like in twenty years' time, give each child a copy of the questions on p. 135 'Life in twenty years' time'. When the children have answered the questions, they could either discuss their answers in small groups, or they could move straight to creative writing. Various subjects could be suggested:

A description of yourself and your life as you think it might actually be in twenty years' time.

A description of yourself and your life as you would like it to be in twenty years' time.

A description of your village/town/city as you think it will be (or as you would like it to be) in twenty years' time. (This could be extended to include painting and model-making.)

The writing should be in the present tense, as if the children were actually writing in twenty years' time. They might find further ideas on what the future might be like in the books about the future and about pollution, conservation and the planet on p. 127.

The future we would like

Divide the class into groups of six to eight children and ask them to discuss the kind of society they would like to see in the future, using the following structure:

1 Each person in the group chooses a goal which they would like to see attained by society in the future. The goals should be specific and achievable.

2 The children consider possible problems and difficulties in achieving their individual goals. For example, space exploration is very expensive, though it does have useful spin-offs in medicine and technology.

3 They consider a society in which all their goals are to be achieved together. Are there conflicts between the different goals? Is there anything which everyone in the group wants?

4 The children try to create a workable set of goals. This will probably involve them in making compromises. They could then consider what steps they would need to take to achieve the goals they want. If some of the groups have chosen goals which are in fact all compatible, they could try and think what other desirable goals might conflict with those they have chosen. The following are examples of pairs of goals which might conflict.

Cars for all: Preservation of the countryside.
Plenty of opportunity for air travel: No airports near people's homes.
Animal rights: Freedom to eat meat.
Large range of consumer goods: No nuclear power or acid rain.
Plenty of money: Plenty of time for leisure.

5 When each group has developed its own plan for the future, the groups should come together and discuss whether all their plans could be implemented at the same time or whether further compromise is necessary. If so, is it more difficult to achieve compromise between groups than it was between individuals?

The future: war or peace?

One topic which may well come up in discussions of possible futures is that of war. This has already been introduced in a rather different context in Section 6. Many children are aware of the possibility of widespread destruction if a major war were to start and especially if nuclear, chemical or biological weapons were used.

The subject of nuclear war is a difficult one. There is little value in frightening children by describing the devastation which can be caused by nuclear weapons. On the other hand, if they are already worried and frightened about the possibility of nuclear war, it may be valuable to give them the opportunity to talk about their fears. If you want to raise the subject of nuclear war, it is probably best to start with an open discussion to see what the children's perceptions of war are. If it then seems appropriate to follow up the discussion, you could encourage the children to imagine firstly a future in which we were involved in nuclear war, and secondly a future in which the threat of war had been removed. You could either simply ask them to express their thoughts and feelings in writing or artwork, or else you could use pp. 136 and 137 to stimulate creative writing and discussion. The pieces of writing reproduced on the sheets are from a lower secondary school in Norfolk.

Follow-up

The children could explore visions of the future by considering how they would act if they were in positions of responsibility, for instance in local government. They could find out what local governments do and then imagine that they are making the policy in their own area.

LIFE IN TWENTY YEARS' TIME

Here are some questions to start you thinking.

In twenty years' time would you expect to:

1 *buy your food from hypermarkets?*
2 *shop without using money?*
3 *watch television holograms?*
4 *have your children educated by computer?*
5 *work a fifteen hour week?*
6 *travel a hundred miles to work?*
7 *wear a gas mask in the street?*
8 *use a videophone?*
9 *wear disposable paper clothes?*
10 *get your basic income from the state, earning extra just to provide luxuries?*
11 *live in a community rather than a family?*
12 *grow your own food using organic methods?*
13 *be a vegetarian?*
14 *travel mainly on state-provided bicycles?*
15 *be severely punished if you caused pollution?*
16 *heat your water using energy from the sun and the wind?*
17 *have birth control imposed by the state?*
18 *have your food and energy supplies rationed by the state?*

THE FUTURE 1

I think everyone would feel really sick before the bomb dropped, sitting in their makeshift shelters not really knowing what was going to happen next. By sick I don't mean frightened: I think everyone would be too busy thinking about the future – their families, their homes – to even consider being frightened.

No, by sick I mean that sinking feeling that you get at the pit of your stomach when you are feeling miserable and someone has died or something like that. At this point I think many people would commit suicide because of the awful prospect of having to live in a world where there are no animals, no plants, no anything – just a long stretch of destruction, ashes and death.

One of the worst times (if you survived the explosion) would be the anticipation of having to wait two long weeks in your shelter. You wouldn't know what the world outside would look like, what people would look like (or you or your family) or how they would react to you.

By the end of these two weeks many more people would have died perhaps from suffocation, disease or, again, suicide.

It would be really terrible to step out of the darkness to find a world shattered with destruction. Houses completely destroyed and people that you once knew maimed or mauled to a state unrecognisable. Wouldn't it be awful to wake up every morning to desolate ground burnt to ashes all around you, no greenery – everything just black – no colour, just black. It's hard to imagine but that's all there would be and probably many people would die from starvation because of this. Also many people would be murdered for food and the world to me wouldn't be worth living in at all.

Fiona

If there is a nuclear war there is nowhere to go. And most of the men and grandads would be called out to fight. Most of us will be killed but some of us might survive. The Queen and the other royal family have places to go to but we haven't. I don't think it's fair. I just hope there is not a war.

Susan

Two girls who are about the same age as you were asked to describe their future – your future – and this is what they wrote. They assumed that the nations of the world would one day use their bombs.

If this happened, how do you imagine the future? Write freely and at length about what you think the world would be like after a nuclear war.

THE FUTURE 2

If all the soldiers throw all the bombs away and all the weapons then there will not be any more wars. Then it might be a peaceful world. If the soldiers did throw the bombs and weapons away they would be unemployed but there will not be in the paper that there is going to be a war in any places. Then there will be no fighting in the world.

Susan

Imagine if Ireland was free of violence – no bombs, no riots, just quietness everywhere. To think you didn't have to search the street every second to find a hiding place in case a gun started spitting out bullets. The world would certainly be a better place, wouldn't it? A much richer one, too. If no weapons were made there would be no poverty or hunger in the poorer countries and the government would spend more money on things like education and work schemes for the unemployed.

There wouldn't be the cloud of fear which rains on some people, either. Everyone would be happy in thought and better physically as well because they would really feel there was a reason to keep fit and to stay alive.

Fiona

The same two girls were asked to imagine a world from which the threat of war had been removed. This is what they wrote. Is this the picture you see? Write freely about what you think the world would be like if the threat of war had been removed.

Get together with a group of your friends and discuss the views of the future you see here and on the other sheet. Which seems more likely? Which would you most like to have? Are there other alternatives? How can you try to create the future you want?

WHAT IS OUR FUTURE?

SECTION 8 CHANGE THROUGH NON-VIOLENT ACTION

This section encourages children to explore the possibilities of peaceful or non-violent action as a means of bringing about change. Suggestions are given for comparing this with some of the violent ways of bringing about change with which the children are probably already familiar. Gandhi and Chavez have been chosen as proponents of non-violent action. Unfortunately it was not so easy to find a female proponent of non-violent action for political change who seemed suitable for study in school with 9–13 year-olds. However, Mother Teresa is an inspiring example of a person working peacefully for change in the care of the poor and the sick, and references are given to some of the many books about her written for children. References are also given to books about another well-known proponent of non-violent action, Martin Luther King, and to books about four people who have used violence as a means for bringing about change: Spartacus, Boudicca, Napoleon and Bolivar.

Lesson ideas for the teacher	Information and activity sheets for the children
8.1 Gandhi	The story of Mahatma Gandhi Gandhi, India and South Africa
8.2 Chavez	The story of Cesar Chavez Chavez and the Californian Strikes
8.3 Violent and non-violent action	
8.4 World Garden	

Further resources
General
Richard B Gregg, *The Power of Nonviolence*, James Clarke, 1960. (T)

Allen and Linda Kirschner (eds), *Blessed are the Peacemakers*, Popular Library, 1971. (T)

Peggy McGeoghan, *Quakers and Peace: Three Hundred Years of Work* (Firbank Folder 2), Friends Education Council, 1978. (T/C)

Peace Pledge Union, *Introduction to Nonviolence and Nonviolent Action.* (T)

Gandhi
Tony Augarde, *Gandhi, a short introduction*, Peace Pledge Union. (T/C)

M K Gandhi, *An Autobiography: The Story of my Experiments with Truth*, Jonathan Cape, 1966. (T)

Michael Gibson, *Gandhi and Nehru*, Wayland, 1981. (C)

Nigel Hunter, *Gandhi*, Wayland, 1986. (C)

F W Rawding, *Gandhi*, Cambridge University Press, 1980. (T/C)

Kathryn Spink, *Gandhi*, Hamish Hamilton, 1984. (C)

Chavez
Christopher Child, *The California Crusade of Cesar Chavez*, Quaker Peace and Service, 1980. (T/C)

Florence M White, *Cesar Chavez: Man of Courage*, Garrard, 1973. (C)

Mother Teresa

Audrey Constant, *In the Streets of Calcutta: The Story of Mother Teresa*, Pergamon, 1980. (C)

Mary Craig, *Mother Teresa*, Hamish Hamilton, 1983. (C)

Sheila M Hobden, *Mother Teresa*, SCM, 1973. (C)

Vanora Leigh, *Mother Teresa*, Wayland, 1985. (C)

Malcolm Muggeridge, *Something Beautiful for God: Mother Teresa of Calcutta*, Collins, 1971. (T)

Anne Sebba, *Mother Teresa*, Franklin Watts, 1982. (C)

Martin Luther King

Nigel Hunter, *Martin Luther King*, Wayland, 1985. (C)

Martin Luther King, *Strength to Love*, Fontana, 1969. (T)

R J Owen, *Free at last: The story of Martin Luther King*, Pergamon Press, 1980. (C)

Peace Pledge Union, Materials from the Peace Education Project:
A Man of Truth (Worksheet for lower secondary)
Assembly Notes for Juniors
Assembly Notes for Seniors
Martin Luther King Poster
Martin Luther King Study Pack
Quotations by and about King
Selections from King's Speeches (Cassette)

Nigel Richardson, *Martin Luther King*, Hamish Hamilton, 1983. (C)

Spartacus

Alfred Duggan, *The Romans*, Brockhampton Press, 1965. (C)

Robin May, *Julius Caesar and the Romans*, Wayland, 1984. (C)

Boudicca (Boadicea)

Plantagenet Somerset Fry, *Boudicca*, W H Allen, 1978. (C)

Lucilla Watson, *Boudicca and the Ancient Britons*, Wayland, 1986. (C)

Napoleon

Neil Grant, *Conquerors*, Macdonald Educational, 1981. (C)

Cleodie Mackinnon, *Great Leaders*, Oxford University Press, 1970. (C)

Anthony Masters, *Napoleon*, Longman, 1981. (C)

L Du Garde Peach, *Napoleon*, Ladybird, 1963. (C)

Stephen Pratt, *Napoleon*, Wayland, 1976. (C)

Simon Bolivar

Neil Grant, *Conquerors*, Macdonald Educational, 1981. (C)

Cleodie MacKinnon, *Great Leaders*, Oxford University Press, 1970. (C)

Start by introducing Gandhi to the children using the account given on p. 143. Older childen can read it for themselves, but with younger children you may want to read it to them or tell them the story in your own words. The account is rather selective in order to encourage the children to find out more about Gandhi. For instance, it does not explain the religious background to the Indian situation, but the children can look up this and other background information with the help of the questions on p. 145 'Gandhi, India and South Africa'.

When the children are familiar with the outline of Gandhi's life, let them divide into groups and ask each group to investigate a particular aspect of his life, using children's encyclopedias and books/booklets such as those listed on p. 139.

Topics for research could include:
  Gandhi's early life (until he went to South Africa)
  His work in South Africa
  The Ashram in Ahmadabad
  The Satyagraha struggle of 1919–22
  The salt march in 1930
  The campaign for the untouchables
  Indian Independence
  The end of Gandhi's life

Each topic could be presented as a piece of writing with illustrations and these could be hung round the wall to form a frieze telling the story of Gandhi's life. The display could include maps of India and South Africa showing places which were important in Gandhi's life.

The story of Gandhi could also be explored using role play. Various different situations and roles could be devised. For example:

1 You and the children are British officials. Thousands of Indians, inspired by Gandhi, are joining the non-violent non-co-operation movement. They are refusing to work in government offices, attend government schools or pay taxes. You are chairing a meeting to discuss what to do about this non-co-operation.

2 You and the children are followers of Gandhi. You are planning to march to the sea to make salt, in defiance of the Salt Acts. You are discussing how to talk to the people through whose villages you will be passing. How will you encourage them to join you? Once you have reached the sea and started making salt, what will you do if the British police arrest you or beat you? How easy do you think it will be to keep to your non-violent principles if people are being violent to you?

THE STORY OF MAHATMA GANDHI

Gandhi was born in India in 1869. His family were Hindus. After studying law in England, Gandhi worked in South Africa. He was shocked at the way Indians who had emigrated there were treated. He believed that they should have equal rights with the whites, and he encouraged them to use non-violent disobedience in protest at their situation. He hoped that in this way they would gain greater equality.

For instance, while Gandhi was in South Africa an Act was passed requiring Indians to carry registration certificates and residence permits wherever they went. This was humiliating and restricted their freedom to move about the country. Gandhi persuaded many of them not to register for their certificates. As a result he and many others were sent to prison. But this did not deter them and they continued to use civil disobedience to try to establish their rights. Gradually their cause became so widely known that the government could no longer ignore them. So in 1914 an Act of Parliament was passed removing many of the regulations against the Indians and admitting the principle of racial equality. General Smuts, who later became Prime Minister of South Africa, said of Gandhi "He never lost his temper or succumbed to hate and preserved his gentle humour in the most trying situations."

When he was forty-four Gandhi returned to India. He soon became the recognised leader of the independence movement which wanted to free India from British rule. Again Gandhi tried to persuade people to work for freedom without using violence. For instance, when he encouraged workers in a cloth factory to strike for an increase in their miserable wages, he laid down four rules:

Never resort to violence.
Never hurt non-strikers.
Never beg for food.
Never give in.

After three weeks the mill owners gave in to the workers and agreed to pay reasonable wages.

In 1930 Gandhi organized a protest against the tax on salt. People felt that this tax was unfair because salt is a basic human necessity. He led a long march to the sea and there the marchers started making their own salt from sea water. This was illegal and many people were arrested. The later attempt to take over the salt works was unsuccessful and many more people were arrested or injured, but they still did not use violence. Their protest resulted in the Salt Acts being re-interpreted. This was an important victory and it gave the people confidence in non-violent campaigns for justice and independence.

Gandhi did not work only for Indian Independence. He believed that India's strength lay in her villages and that these should be self-sufficient units where everyone had a say in how things were run. He thought that all people should be treated equally, regardless of sex, religion or caste. He put these ideas into practice in his ashram in Ahmadabad. This was a community which led a simple life of prayer, study, manual work and helping local people. Gandhi dressed very simply, wearing cotton that he had spun himself. Even when he was invited to have tea with the King and Queen at Buckingham Palace, he went in his Indian peasant clothes with sandals and a shawl.

Gandhi was a deeply religious man. He had great humility and unshakeable courage. He believed firmly in the ways of justice, truth and love and was able to influence millions just by his personal example. Sometimes when people were using violence he would fast and refuse to eat until the violence stopped. People respected him so greatly that they made peace with each other rather than let Gandhi starve himself to death.

India did eventually free itself from British rule, but to Gandhi's sorrow the country was divided so that the Muslims were in the separate state of Pakistan. Soon after, in 1948, Gandhi was assassinated by a Hindu extremist who was angry at Gandhi's defence of Muslims. People throughout the world mourned his death, and his example has influenced many.

GANDHI, INDIA AND SOUTH AFRICA

When you have listened to or read the story of Gandhi, try to find answers to the following questions:

1 What is a Hindu? Find out about Hindu beliefs and customs and about the caste system.

2 What is a Muslim? Find out about Muslim beliefs and customs.

3 What kind of climate does South Africa have? What grows there?

4 Can you find out anything about the Indians living in South Africa?

5 In what part of India is Ahmadabad? (It can also be spelt Ahmedabad.) What is the climate like there? What grows there?

6 What is civil disobedience?
Try to think of an occasion where civil disobedience has been used in Britain. What were people trying to achieve by breaking the law?
Did they succeed in any of their aims?
Did they influence public opinion?

Start by introducing Chavez to the children using the account given on p. 148. Older childen can read it for themselves, but with younger children you may want to read it to them or tell them the story in your own words. The children can then try to answer the questions on p. 150 'Chavez and the Californian Strikes'. When they have done this they should discuss their answers in small groups. They can also attempt to find out more about Chavez for themselves (see p. 139), though there is not a great deal of information readily available in Britain.

The story of Chavez could also be explored using drama. Various different situations and roles could be devised, for example:

1 The class are farmworkers and you are the union agitator. You want them all to go on strike, but some of them are worried about the risks. Not only will they lose their pay, they may also lose their homes and even be beaten and sent to prison.

2 You and the children are followers of Chavez. You have been on strike for some time and you are feeling desperate because the grape growers still have not given you what you want. You are discussing whether you should resort to violence or whether it is better to keep to the peaceful methods you have been using up to now.

THE STORY OF CESAR CHAVEZ

Cesar Chavez was born in 1927 in Arizona, USA. His parents were Mexicans. When he was ten his family lost their farm because of the economic depression. So they were forced to join the penniless migrants who wandered all over California in search of farm work. Chavez describes this period:

"When we moved to California, we would work after school. Sometimes we wouldn't go. 'Following the crops', we missed much school. Trying to get enough money to stay alive the following winter, the whole family picking apricots, walnuts, prunes. We were pretty new, we had never been migratory workers. We were taken advantage of quite a bit by the labour contractor."

The migrant families lived in appalling conditions, in shacks with no running water and infested with lice. They worked long hours, often exposed to poisonous pesticides and dangerous machinery. Their pay was so low that the whole family, including the children, had to work. The experience of poverty and racialism that the Chavez family and their fellow workers had to endure in the years that followed began to stir Chavez to rebellion. He describes a small incident:

"We went through Indio, California. Along the highway there were signs in most of the small restaurants that said 'White Trade Only'. My Dad read English, but he didn't really know the meaning. He went in to get some coffee . . . for my mother. He asked us not to come in, but we followed him anyway. And this young waitress said, "We don't serve Mexicans here. Get out of here." I was there, and I saw it and heard it. She paid no more attention. I'm sure for the rest of her life she never thought of it again. But every time we thought of it, it hurt us. So we got back in the car and we had a difficult time trying – in fact, we never got the coffee. These are sort of unimportant, but they're . . . you remember 'em very well."

When he was twenty-one Chavez married a fellow migrant worker, who was to help him in his struggle to improve the lot of the farmworkers. He became friendly with his parish priest and learned about Gandhi and Martin Luther King. He was inspired by their ideas of peaceful change. In 1962 he began to organize a union of farmworkers through which he hoped they could try to improve their conditions. The union agreed to use only non-violent methods. Three years later the multi-racial United Farm Workers launched a strike. The workers in the vineyards of the San Joaquin Valley in California walked out because the growers refused to listen to their requests for more pay.

The growers responded to the strike with violence. Armed guards were posted at the fields to prevent pickets talking to strike breakers. Strike leaders were evicted from the camps where they lived and were often arrested. Many ranch foremen carried guns and hit, kicked and spat on the pickets. Chavez insisted that the strikers should not use violence in return, and the strike remained peaceful. Public sympathy for the farmworkers grew and a boycott was planned. People were asked not to buy grapes unless they bore the union's Aztec eagle trademark, and this boycott eventually achieved support in many parts of the world.

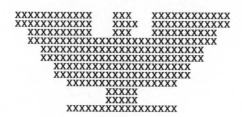

This page may be photocopied

In 1967 the strikers marched three hundred miles to the capital of California to present the farmworkers' case to the Governor. During the march one of the many grape growing corporations signed an agreement with the union. This was an important victory for the farmworkers. However, when the marchers reached the capital the Governor was not there.

After this some union members began to get impatient and felt that Chavez's non-violent methods were not producing results fast enough, so they began using violence. Chavez was worried and early in 1968 announced that he was fasting as an act of penance for the union's move towards violence. The fast attracted national publicity and drew the union together again. After twenty-five days Chavez ended his fast and a huge crowd assembled to hear him. He was very weak so someone else read out the speech he had written. In it Chavez said "I am convinced that the truest act of courage . . . is to sacrifice ourselves in a totally non-violent struggle for justice." Senator Robert Kennedy, who had come to join the gathering, said "I am here out of respect for one of the great heroes of our time." A feast of thanksgiving followed and the strikers promised not to use violence again.

In 1970, after further struggle, final contracts were signed with the major grape growers. The contracts included provision for a fair basic wage, a ban on child labour and an agreement not to use the most dangerous pesticides. The struggle was not over, but the first years show something of the strength of this non-violent campaign. In 1975 the United Farmworkers Union of America adopted a resolution confirming their commitment to non-violence.

"This organization pledges to live by the creed of non-violence as proclaimed by Jesus Christ and prescribed by our teacher M K Gandhi and Dr. Martin Luther King. . . . If to build our union requires the deliberate taking of human life . . . then we choose not to see our union built."

Chavez added to this:

"Truth is justice and if you stick to that you can overturn mountains. It's all a question of what we are doing on earth. Are we here to make money? Are we here to get what we can for ourselves? Or are we here to do something for our fellow men?"

CHAVEZ AND THE CALIFORNIAN STRIKES

When you have listened to or read the story of Chavez, try to find answers to the following questions:

1 *Where is California?*
   What is the climate like there?
2 *What is a penniless migrant?*
             a picket?
             a foreman?
3 *What is racialism?*
   Can you think of an example of racialism in Britain?
4 *What are pesticides?*
   In what ways can they be harmful?
5 *Why do you think Chavez and the strikers won so much support?*
6 *Try to imagine that you are one of the migrant farmworkers.*
   a) *How do you feel about the way you are being treated?*
   b) *Why do your fellow workers want to go on strike?*
   c) *Do you want to join them? Why, or why not?*
   d) *If you go on strike, do you want to use violence?*
   e) *What might be the advantages of using violence?*
   f) *What might be the disadvantages of using violence?*
8 *Try to think of a recent strike in this country.*
   a) *What was it about?*
   b) *Was there any violence?*
      If yes, who was involved in it?
      Did anyone speak out against the violence?
   c) *Did the strikers get what they wanted?*
      If yes, how?
   d) *In what ways do you think the strike was justified or unjustified?*
   e) *Do you take sides in strikes?*
      If yes, do you find out all you can about the strike first?

8.3　VIOLENT AND NON-VIOLENT ACTION

The idea of working peacefully for change can be explored further by considering people such as Jesus, Martin Luther King and Mother Teresa. Their methods could be contrasted with those of people who have used violence to achieve their aims. There are many people who could serve as examples here, such as Spartacus, Boudicca (Boadicea), Napoleon and Simon Bolivar. When the children have read about some of these people, using encyclopedias and books such as those listed on p. 139–140, you could have a discussion:

Why do you think violent action has so often been used in the past?
Can you think of other examples of violent action?
What do people find difficult about using non-violent methods?
Where has violence succeeded? Failed?
What counts as success? As failure?
What are the real costs of violence? Non-violence?

8.4 WORLD GARDEN*

'World Garden' draws together some of the themes of the book. Through art and drama it encourages children to think imaginatively about the future and their role in shaping it. It also provides another opportunity to look at how conflicts can develop and be resolved, and at the consequences of violent and non-violent solutions.

'World Garden' is the name given to a play area such as a deserted garden, a park or a piece of waste ground where local children go to play. Start by asking the children to imagine what they would like to see in such a garden. They might come up with suggestions such as a shrubbery, a pond, a summer house, a playground, a football pitch or a car dump.

Art

Ask the children to paint a large pictorial map of the garden for the classroom wall. A few of them could draw the outline, and sections could then be filled in by small groups. The children could paint and cut out pictures of themselves and put them on the map.

Drama

The children start by imagining games they could play in the garden. They then divide into groups and play some of these games. Try to encourage the more imaginative games. At first the groups play happily alongside each other, but after a little while you should introduce some event or restriction which might lead to conflict between different groups. For instance, you could give each group its own area: one might have the playground and the summerhouse, another the grassed area and another the shrubbery. One area could be much bigger and more attractive than the others. You should whisper to each group that the other groups are hostile and liable to throw stones if their boundaries are crossed. You then need to set the scene for an 'It isn't fair' cry, perhaps by introducing a rain storm or setting up an ice cream stall in one of the areas. Arguments are likely to develop and at a suitable moment you should stop the drama and continue the story through discussion.

Discussion

How and why did the arguments start?
What are people feeling?
What might happen next?
How could the conflict be resolved?

The last question could be tackled by having a 'brainstorm' (see p. 128). All suggestions, whether naive, violent or constructive, should be accepted. You could then ask the children which of the solutions involve shifting the responsibility on to someone else. ('Call the police' or 'Let the parents sort it out' would come into this category.) Suggest that they should concentrate on solutions where they themselves take the responsibility. What would be the consequences of the different solutions? Which would make the garden a good place to play? Is there any solution which everyone would be happy with? Are there similarities between the situation in the garden and situations in the wider world (such as conflicts over resources)?

*This activity is partly based on the 'World Park' idea of John McConnell's described in *The Friend*, 2 October 1981.

Art

Ask the children to paint two pictures, one showing the garden as it might be if the groups continue arguing and maybe fighting, and the other showing how the garden might be if the groups decide to co-operate and perhaps work together to improve the garden. (If they pooled their resources they might, for instance, build some model boats to sail on the pond.) The paintings could be displayed beside the pictorial map of the garden to illustrate how our choices can affect our future.

APPENDIX 1

ASSEMBLIES, POEMS AND SONGS

This appendix contains outlines of two assemblies which have been used successfully in schools. The poems and songs can also be used at other times.

UNITED NATIONS DAY ASSEMBLY

One of the children reads this Chinese Proverb:

If there be righteousness in the heart
There will be beauty in the character.
If there is beauty in the character
There will be harmony in the home.
If there is harmony in the home
There will be order in the nation.
When there is order in each nation,
There will be peace in the world.

The teacher or another child enlarges on this with a few words based on the following:

Peace in the world is the responsibility of everyone. We must begin with ourselves. Each of us has to be prepared to be just, kind and loving to all. A stone falling into a pool sends ripples which affect the whole pool. Similarly, our behaviour can affect all whom we meet, and they in turn affect those they meet. The more stones and the larger the pool, the greater the number of ripples. Thus from small beginnings peace could spread throughout the world.

End by singing *One Man's Hands*.

ARMISTICE DAY SERVICE

This is an assembly which was presented to the lower part of a comprehensive school in Norfolk. Children were used as readers but the linking commentary was spoken by a member of staff. The assembly seeks to present to children the facts of war through poetry and song, prose and music. It brings out the futility rather than the glory of war and presents the idea that throughout history the ordinary person has been able to see no alternative to his involvement in it. There is a danger that such an assembly is seen to denigrate those millions who have died and still continue to die. However, the assembly tries to involve the children in an experience which leads them to think about the issues. It did, in fact, serve to stimulate discussion in many classrooms during the day which followed, and thus there were opportunities to talk about various aspects of war. However, the assembly could be extended to include other aspects of a soldier's life by adding further readings and songs, such as some of those on pp. 116 and 158. The sources of the poems and songs used in this assembly are given on p. 158.

As it stands, this assembly is not suitable for children under twelve. However, it could be adapted for younger children by substituting other readings and songs such as some of those listed on pp. 116 and 158.

Today, the 11th of November, is Armistice Day when once again we remember those who died in two World Wars. This time we would like to look at the soldier through the ages – the universal soldier. He is the representative of millions of soldiers who have triumphed and died, shown cowardice or heroism, fought for cause or country, volunteered or been pressed into the army. Through our readings this morning we would like to show his humour, his battles and his sacrifices.

The Universal Soldier stands

When we say the word 'soldier' it conjures up uniforms, flags, beating drums and wild charges. In fact these play about as much part in a soldier's life as Sports Day or a school concert plays in yours. A soldier's life in peacetime may be boring, repetitive and miserable. Our first soldier is a Roman and . . .

He is handed a spear and a shield

He is cold, wet and bad-tempered on Hadrian's Wall guarding the newly-conquered British from the Picts and Scots. The poem is called *Roman Wall Blues* and it is followed by the song *Universal Soldier*.

Roman Wall Blues

Universal Soldier

We should never forget what we owe to the Universal Soldier. He guards and protects. In Northern Ireland he still dies today, though he is not to blame for the situation and may not fully understand it. Nor should we forget the price that he has to pay. War is not only a matter of victory or death – it often entails terrible injuries.

The Universal Soldier is given crutches

The song dates from the 18th century and tells how a wife feels when her husband returns injured from the wars. It is called *Johnny, I hardly knew you.*

Johnny, I hardly knew you read by a girl accompanied by flute.

The soldier is trained to kill. He is given a spear or gun or bayonet and taught the most effective way to deliver death. For most of us the idea of killing is not easy and when the Universal Soldier is given his bayonet he has to be given his instructions.

The Universal Soldier is given a bayonet

The next two readings show the two sides of this process. Firstly, in a piece by Brecht, the soldier is brutally conditioned to kill. In the second item, *The Happy Warrior*, we feel the reality when the bayonet has to be used on a living man.

Extract from *The Caucasian Chalk Circle* by Brecht.

The Happy Warrior.

In the twentieth century, wars took on a different character. The number of killed and wounded multiplied in a way which is difficult to understand. We can take in one death, but a million? 15,400 – the size of a Norwich City football crowd – died at the Battle of Inkerman during the Crimean War in 1854. Half a million died at Gallipoli. $2\frac{1}{2}$ million Germans died on the Eastern Front in the last World War – along with 7 million Russians. The Universal Soldier had to adapt himself to heavy artillery, tanks and gas.

The Universal Soldier is given a gas mask, together with instructions on how to put it on.

You have 28 seconds to get that mask on yer.
Take any more and you're sure a gonner,

My 'orrible little man.
So don't stand about like a silly great lass
You've got 28 seconds when you hear the word 'gas'.

Gas – the word struck terror and against this weapon men might show courage but there was very little glory. The next poem describes a gas attack, and the poet – who died in the First World War – calls it *Dulce et decorum est pro patria mori* which means 'It is sweet and noble to die for your native land.' He warns the children of the next generation that such war is not glorious.

Dulce et decorum est

What now for the Universal Soldier? Weapons are measured in megatons – a megaton is equivalent to a million tons of TNT. What will the soldier be given to combat the nuclear threat? The next song gives an answer though it is not a pleasant one. It is called *Fifteen Million Plastic Bags* and was written by Adrian Mitchell. (Alternatively you could use *The Sun is Burning* by Ian Campbell.)

Fifteen Million Plastic Bags
or
The Sun is Burning

We shall end with the song *Strangest Dream*.

Strangest Dream

Sources of readings and songs

United Nations Day Assembly

Peter Smith (ed), *Faith, Folk & Clarity*, Galliard, 1967.
 Alex Comfort & Pete Seeger, *One Man's Hands*.

Armistice Day Assembly

Geoffrey Summerfield (ed), *Voices 1*, Penguin, 1968.
 W H Auden, *Roman Wall Blues*.
CND, *Songs for Peace*, CND.
 Ian Campbell, *The Sun is Burning*.
 Ed McCurdy, *Strangest Dream*.
 Buffy Sainte Marie, *Universal Soldier*.
Karl Dallas, *The Cruel Wars*, Wolfe.
 Traditional, *Johnny, I hardly knew you*.
Bertolt Brecht, *The Caucasian Chalk Circle*, Methuen, 1963.
 Scene 3: dialogue between Corporal and Ironshirts
I M Parsons (ed), *Men Who March Away*, Chatto and Windus, 1978.
 Wilfred Owen, *Dulce et Decorum Est.*
 Herbert Read, *The Happy Warrior.*
Phillip Larkin (ed), Oxford Book of Twentieth Century English Verse, OUP, 1973.
 Adrian Mitchell, *Fifteen million plastic bags.*

Other songs and poems which relate to themes dealt with in the book (see also p. 96)

CND, *Songs for Peace*, CND.
 Bob Dylan, *Blowing in the Wind.*
 Pete Seeger, *Where have all the flowers gone?*
 Pete Seeger and Lee Hays, *If I had a hammer.*
Peter Smith (ed), *Faith, Folk and Clarity*, Galliard, 1967.
 Sydney Carter, *When I needed a neighbour.*
 Fred Dallas, *The Family of Man.*
 Pete Seeger and Lee Hays, *If I had a hammer.*
Kevin Mayhew (ed), *Twentieth Century Folk Hymnal*, K Mayhew.
Vol 1: Sydney Carter, *When I needed a neighbour.*
 Sebastian Temple, *Make me a channel of your peace.*
Vol 2: Sebastian Temple, *Lord we pray for golden peace.*
Janet Adam-Smith (ed), *Faber Book of Children's Verse*, Faber, 1953.
 Lord Byron, *The Destruction of Sennacherib.*
 W B Yeats, *An Irish Airman Foresees His Death.*
Alan Brownjohn (ed), *First I Say This*, Hutchinson Educational,1969.
 Anon, *As I walked out in the streets of Laredo.*
 Anon, *The Rebel Soldier.*
A E Housman, *Collected Poems*, Jonathan Cape, 1939.
 Epitaph on an army of mercenaries
 Farewell to a name and number
 Grenadier
 My dreams are of a field afar
 Oh stay at home, my lad, and plough
John Rowe Townsend (ed), *Modern Poetry*, OUP, 1971.
 R N Currey, *Unseen Fire.*
Siegfried Sassoon, *Collected Poems*, Faber, 1984.
 Counter Attack
 Trench Duty

APPENDIX 2

A SMALL SELECTION OF CHILDREN'S FICTION

Below are listed some stories which relate to themes dealt with in this book.

Nina Bawden, *Carrie's War*, Puffin, 1974.

Malcolm J Bosse, *Ganesh*, Puffin, 1984.

Alice Rowe Burks, *Leela and the Leopard Hunt*, Methuen, 1983.

John Christopher, *White Mountains*, Hamlyn, 1976.

Eleanor Coerr, *Sadaka and the One Thousand Paper Cranes*, Hodder, 1983.

Susan Cooper, *Dawn of Fear*, Puffin, 1974.

Gillian Cross, *The Runaway*, Magnet Books, 1986.

Andrew Davies, *Conrad's War*, Hippo Books, 1980.

Anita Desai, *The Peacock Garden*, Heinemann, 1979.

Peter Dickinson, *The Devil's Children*, Puffin, 1972.

Tony Drake, *Playing It Right*, Puffin, 1981.

Geraldine Kaye, *Comfort Herself*, Magnet Books, 1986.

Judith Kerr, *When Hitler stole Pink Rabbit*, Armada Lions, 1974.

Clive King, *Stig of the Dump*, Puffin, 1970.

Jan Mark, *Thunder and Lightnings*, Puffin, 1978.

Ron Morton, *The Squeeze*, Hamish Hamilton, 1984.

Jan Needle, *My Mate Shofiq*, Armada Lions, 1979.

Hans Peter Richter, *Friederich*, Longman, 1971.

Ian Serraillier, *The Silver Sword*, Puffin, 1970.

Ivan Southall, *Josh*, Puffin, 1974.

APPENDIX 3

USEFUL ADDRESSES

British Film Institute Education Department
81 Dean Street, London W1V 6AA

Central America Information Service
1 Amwell Street, London EC1R 1UL

Centre for Global Education
University of York, Heslington, York YO1 5DD

Centre for Peace Studies
St Martin's College, Lancaster LA1 3JD

Centre for World Development Education
Regent's College, Inner Circle, Regent's Park, London NW1 4NS

Concord Films Council
201 Felixstowe Road, Ipswich, Suffolk IP3 9BJ

Council for Education in World Citizenship
19 Tudor Street, London EC4Y 0DJ

Council for Environmental Education
University of Reading, London Road, Reading RG1 5AQ

E A R O
The Resource Centre, Back Hill, Ely, Cambs. CB7 4DA

Friends Book Centre
Friends House, Euston Road, London NW1 2BJ

Housmans Bookshop
5 Caledonian Road, Kings Cross, London N1 9DY

Imperial War Museum
Lambeth Road, London SE1 6HZ

International and Multicultural Education Project
Jordanhill College of Education, Southbrae Drive, Glasgow G13 1PF

Irish Council of Churches Peace Education Programme
48 Elmwood Avenue, Belfast BT9 6AZ

National Association of Development Education Centres
6 Endsleigh Street, London WC1H 0DX

One World Trust
24 Palace Chambers, Bridge Street, London SW1A 2JT

Oxfam Education Department
274 Banbury Road, Oxford OX2 7DZ

Pax Christi Peace Education Centre
St Francis of Assisi Centre, Pottery Lane, London W11 4NQ

Peace Education Project (Peace Pledge Union)
6 Endsleigh Street, London WC1H 0DX

Pictorial Charts Educational Trust
27 Kirchen Road, London W13 0UD

Play for Life
31B Ipswich Road, Norwich NR2 2LN

Quaker Peace and Service
Friends House, Euston Road, London NW1 2BJ

United Nations Association
3 Whitehall Court, London SW1A 2EL

World Education Berkshire
Haymill Centre, 112 Burnham Lane, Slough SL1 6LZ

INDEX OF THEMES.

Pages dealing with some important themes are given below. See also Index of School Subjects.

INDEX OF SCHOOL SUBJECTS

The principal pages relevant to various school subjects are given below.

INDEX OF INFORMATION AND ACTIVITY SHEETS

DATE DUE